Take your Mary Baker city mix and mix yourself a city
       to a plan,
Take the super giant pack and make a few identicities
       while you can.
And as you sterilise and standardise, and cauterise
       the ancient city's ills,
You'll find the architects and planners have all
       saved themselves a cottage in the hills.

from *The Mary Baker City Mix* by Alex Glasgow 1971

Design Education

problem solving and visual experience

Peter Green

B.T Batsford Limited   London

© Peter Green 1974
First published 1974
Reprinted 1978 (first paperback edition)

ISBN 0 7134 2325 0

Designed by Elsa Willson
Filmset by Servis Filmsetting Limited, Manchester
Printed and bound in Great Britain by
The Anchor Press Ltd, Tiptree, Essex
for the publishers B T Batsford Limited
4 Fitzhardinge Street, London W1H 0AH

Contents

Acknowledgment

As with much of the design process itself, this book is the result of collective, corporate activity. Numerous groups of people have worked together in exploring design education methods and studying how we can become critically involved in the study of our environment. The authorship is therefore in some ways a group process and I am anxious to recognise the helpful contributions I have received from friends and colleagues.

I would like to thank all the students with whom I have worked. These include serving teachers on courses, post-graduate art teacher training students and secondary school pupils. They have all helped develop ideas and have provided the testing ground for many of the exploratory programmes of work.

In more specific and personal terms I would like to thank all the staff of the Department of Teacher Training, at the former Hornsey College of Art, for their friendship and constant tolerant help.

I also acknowledge with special gratitude the help given by: David Hayles for help in three-dimensional work and for working with me on so many teachers' courses; Stuart Michaels for taking many of the photographs; Erik Sonntag, Director of Teachers Courses in design education at Hornsey, for generously lending work; Simon Green for contributing drawings and for much valuable help; Innumerable teachers on in-service and vacation courses, especially those from Cumberland and Northumberland, who were involved in several happy experiments; Michael Tiddy, art adviser, and Jeff Coxon, technical studies adviser, for Cumberland Education Authority, who have given so much friendly support.

The following education authority advisers for involving me in courses or for giving help and advice: Bernard Aylward (Leicestershire), Charles Barnham (Oxfordshire), Bob Clement (Devon), Derek Jones-Darlington (Oldham), Peter Sellwood (Dorset), Derek Peck (Derbyshire), Leo Walmsley (Bromley), Geoffrey Sutcliffe (Cheshire), Geoffrey Drewitt, Jim Mackenzie (Northumberland), Bill Howes-Bassett (Newham), Maurice Barrett (Redbridge), and many others.

Teachers attending Art Centre Courses at Hornsey, especially Phil Thompson and Bill Read; Jon Tacey for his influence in some early thinking on structural problem solving, and for lending work; Marshall Mateer and Philip Tootell, colleagues in teacher training, who have helped by lending work; John Prescott Thomas of the BBC who, in working with to produce the *Look Out* series, helped me develop and clarify so many ideas; Alex Glasgow for giving permission for part of his song, *The Mary Baker City Mix*, to be reproduced, and for incidentally presenting the *Look Out* series with such livliness; The publishers of *Alex Glasgow an Anthology*, Robbins Music Corporation distributed by Frances Day and Hunter; Michael Swain, Head of Creative Activities Department, Sheredes School, Hoddesdon, Hertfordshire, for lending me a draft scheme of his GCE/CSE Examination proposals; The Oxford Delegacy of Local Examinations for kindly giving permission to reproduce extracts from the first 'A' Level GCE Design paper; The Art Staff at Uppingham School, Rutland for allowing me to include an example of a student's work from the first Oxford GCE 'A' Level paper.

The following Education Authorities for kindly lending plans and photographs of secondary school design centres and art/craft departments: Cumberland Education Committee, Derbyshire Education Committee, Leicestershire Education Department, The County Borough of Oldham Education Authority, Oxfordshire County Education Department, Peterborough Education Committee.

I would also like to thank, for various help, the staff of the Jack Hunt School Peterborough; Edgar Rogers of Stanborough School, Welwyn, Hertfordshire; Gareth Morse of Henbury School, Bristol; the art staff at Creighton School, Muswell Hill, North London; and Laurie Harper of Moray House College of Education, Edinburgh.

Marks and Spencer Limited for permission to take photographs at their Wood Green branch; Messrs Dent & Co Limited, publishers for permission to reproduce details from Shepherds Glossary of Graphic Signs and Symbols.

Of the local teachers who have contributed so much I must specially thank Eileen Rapley for the major work and considerable help she has given and the way she has carried out practical problem solving projects and helped on teaching programmes.

Unfortunately, late in the production schedule, severe economies of scale imposed strict selective editing, forcing us to exclude work that had been kindly lent. To all those unseen contributors I would like to express my sincere thanks.

Finally I would like to thank Elsa Willson, typographer, for designing the layout and jacket of the book with such care and skill; and Thelma M. Nye for once again editing with patience and guiding the book through many difficulties.

Highgate 1974   PG

General introduction to design education

Part 1

Social, educational and industrial background

We live in a man-made environment and someone is responsible for the form of things around us and consequently the very quality of our lives. The decision maker, with these responsibilities, may be a designer, architect, town planner, television producer, advertiser or local authority officer.

Our environment can be described as all that surrounds us other than ourselves — not only buildings and man-made objects but films and television, sounds and smells, magazines and advertisements, in fact all that is received by our senses. An example of the scope and impact of the man-made environment may be seen if we consider, for example, how much television we watch (eighteen hours a week — nearly ten years of our lives), or how many visual advertisements we see (about a thousand a day).

We are often insensitive to the visual appearance, and subsequent effect upon us, of our surroundings. Urban areas are frequently chaotic jumbles which we tolerate, suffer, try to ignore, or take for granted. Such disorder will continue unless we can make some articulate and informed response to the surroundings imposed on us.

We need to look in new and critical ways at the changing world and become aware, not only of its visual appearance, but more important, the forces at work behind it which shape the man-made environment.

Design education is not about imposing 'good taste' or buying wisely. It is more concerned with developing a critical understanding of human needs and gaining experience in evaluating whether these needs have been met adequately. There is no such thing as good or bad design, but rather appropriate or inappropriate, efficient or inefficient solutions to problems.

The 'design process' is not just a matter of shaping the appearance of things around us but also of shaping the way we live. In a pre-industrial society natural forces were significant 'designers'. A landscape was formed and affected by the elements and such action ultimately determined where man could live or farm, where he could mine and so on. Man himself can now shape large areas of his environment, determining not only the way he himself lives but also the pattern of life for thousands of other people as well.

Industrial production systems can manufacture and multiply individual decisions into a mass form, touching all our lives. It would therefore seem important to see the design process not as 'accidentally inspired artistry' but as a responsible activity in which we are all involved. Design decisions in a pre-industrial system were either made to individual order or affected the lives of relatively few people. One of the significant characteristics of mass production and the mass media is that designers' solutions are inflicted on us all and we become reluctant consumers, too often passive or inarticulate in our response.

Responsible design solutions in an industrial society are obviously not the result of casual intuitive activity. The designer in a mass society cannot afford such luxury. He has to assess carefully the needs of many people and consider other frequently conflicting requirements for which he has to propose efficient solutions.

All design decisions relate to the problem-solving process: the basic process of identifying a problem or need and then testing a proposed solution. Such a process is clearly close to the fundamental processes of creative education and our daily lives. Every day we arrange things around us in ways which are really practical solutions to design problems — we arrange tools on benches, utensils in the kitchen, clothes in drawers, so that they can be used efficiently. Experience of problem solving is common to education, the design process and daily life, and is therefore central to any ideas related to design education.

Two other considerations are also of immediate relevance to the nature of design education. These are the characteristics of change brought about by scientific and technological developments and the increasing range of human choice making which naturally follows.

Possibly for the first time in human history the rate of social, economic and technical change creates a situation where the lessons of the immediate past may no longer be relevant. We therefore need to look for new relationships and new processes of learning, experience and evaluation.

With rapidly advancing technology we now have to handle, in the space of a few years, the kind of adaptation which used to be handled as one generation passed into another.

Such a rate of change, with all its implications, has many immediate effects on our attitudes to the processes of education relevant to design education. New discoveries bring new knowledge leading to an 'information overload'.

Traditional systems whereby a teacher represented a body of knowledge to be learned are no longer necessarily viable. Individual knowledge can no longer cover the expansion of ideas and technical information. New experiences, simultaneously confronting both adult and pupil, require learning relationships based on mutual discovery and experience. We need to adopt methods of learning which are flexible, to be able to identify new needs and problems and to propose and discover relevant solutions.

If design education is to concern itself with the new technology it cannot be restrained with inherited aesthetic cultural values or imposed laws of absolute values. Adaptable systems of evaluation should be relevant to each widely differing problem. Such critical evaluation stems from a thorough understanding of the nature of the problem to be solved and the testing of the proposed solution in terms of the initially identified needs.

Having given some thought to the impact of the rate of social and technological change we must also consider the subsequent growth of choice making, the amount and range of which is increasing in all areas of human activity.

To appreciate fully the extension of the frontiers of human choice making it is necessary to think not only of economic factors. We travel further, we can choose where to go, we have social mobility and have more choice in the nature of our employment and where we live. Within new freedoms we can choose how to behave and how to dress, for formal social patterns have broken down considerably. Scientific discoveries and psychological developments have helped to provide more choice in moral codes and more freedom in physical relations. We can choose what to watch, listen to, read, surround ourselves with and, most significantly, enjoy rapidly increasing 'free choice time'. We are therefore being confronted with new decisions — decisions which a previous generation did not necessarily have to make. There was a certain suspect security in earlier non-industrial society where choice making was limited to knowing what was right or wrong and having little free time in which to choose what to do.

Education, in many instances, tends to give solutions and tidy facts rather than equip us for the more flexible solving of new problems. We are not going to be able to deal with the growth of decision making unless we have had experience of making realistic decisions ourselves, and of testing the effiency of these decisions. The need for such practical problem-solving experience is crucial and a central part of all design education.

In many ways industrialisation and mass production mean more choices, more things to buy and more money with which to buy them. Decision-making zones proliferate on the one hand but on the other hand there are fewer choices. In this context, if education encourages choice making, it is in a way subversive — making people dissatisfied with the limits of choice.

Mass production means that we have no say in the design and manufacturing stages of commodities — all the choices are made, except the final one of buying, and this is influenced by such elements as fashion and advertising.

However we do have to make more decisions ourselves, but the decisions made on our behalf are far-reaching and ubiquitous.

As consumers of the mass designers' and

planners' products we need to be articulate and active in our response. So many design solutions have visual form that what is now required is a visually literate community capable of understanding the reasons for the visual forms that surround us.

Our major traditions in education revolve around literacy and numeracy: little emphasis has been placed on the need to develop a genuine educational language of visual form. Such visual literacy is a further central characteristic of design education.

Often intelligence is acknowledged only when it is in written form or when connected with mathematics or science. Equally 'creativity' is recognised only in traditional form, as when using paint or clay. Education should be dynamic, responding to the changing needs of young people. It may be feasible here to try to establish a parallel between the role of the teacher and the designer. Like the designer, the educator needs to accurately identify the needs of the consumer. Having established the priority of requirements both set out to provide experiences and solutions that are relevant to these needs. In such a context design education is not yet another academic body of information but rather a constantly changing series of opportunities to learn through experience of valid decision-making activity.

It is important to stress that 'design' is not just the visual part of the production process added on, nor is the designer just a 'visual stylist' — the man who adds the looks. The designer is the decision maker determining all aspects of the environment. The appearance of an object is rather like the tip of an iceberg: the process of design involves much more than the outer appearance. Design is a fundamental process involving many people and vitally concerned with meeting human needs efficiently. To illustrate the total significance of the revolution in design technology we could say that the object of it is to achieve more with less. Such an idea I think summarises the potential breadth of the design process, in social and economic terms.

The role of the artist in the twentieth century is clearly changing. The romantic concept of the esoteric fine artist is largely an anachronism. A potentially more acceptable role would be to see the artist either as the responsible designer of our environment or as the efficient mass communicator. Such a description overstates the situation, but possibly illustrates the developing nature of the artist's role. What is significant is that words such as 'responsible' and 'efficient' begin to emerge, indicating the social responsibility of the designer/artist in a mass society. No longer do we see the designer as an isolated, inspired individual working on his own spectacular activity like the 'artist'. With the growth of technology and science, economic complexity and mass consumption, the designer more and more becomes part of a team of specialists.

Similarly the design process now includes varied disciplines from engineering to science, from psychology to mathematics.

Design is a human activity in which everyone is involved; it it a process of identifying problems and needs and establishing critical priorities. It requires research, data collection, organisation of resources and rational analysis and measurement. And as a solution evolves, by rational synthesis or practical trial and error, it takes on a form and has to be tested and evaluated.

This universal process of problem solving is what design is about. We are all involved in the critical creative process of design.

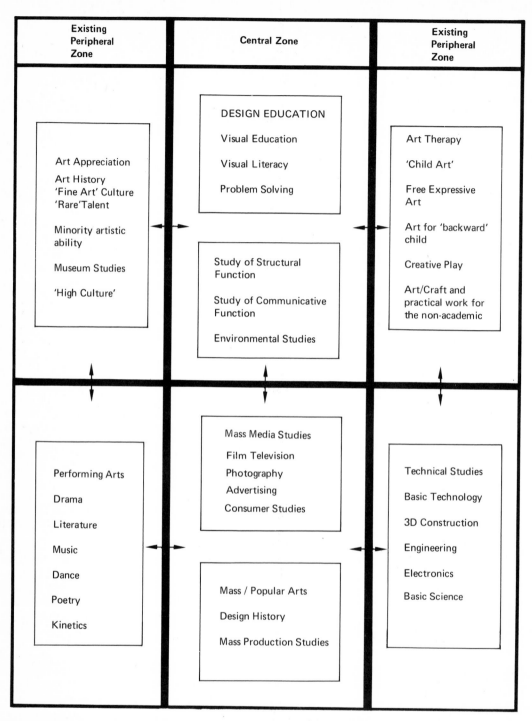

Existing Peripheral Zone	Central Zone	Existing Peripheral Zone
Art Appreciation Art History 'Fine Art' Culture 'Rare' Talent Minority artistic ability Museum Studies 'High Culture'	DESIGN EDUCATION Visual Education Visual Literacy Problem Solving Study of Structural Function Study of Communicative Function Environmental Studies	Art Therapy 'Child Art' Free Expressive Art Art for 'backward' child Creative Play Art/Craft and practical work for the non-academic
Performing Arts Drama Literature Music Dance Poetry Kinetics	Mass Media Studies Film Television Photography Advertising Consumer Studies Mass / Popular Arts Design History Mass Production Studies	Technical Studies Basic Technology 3D Construction Engineering Electronics Basic Science

1   Central function of design education: adding to what is already offered, crossing discipline barriers and connecting subjects.

It is important to stress the nature of design education, adding to that which exists rather than re-placing existing work, though it may be that existing activities are too narrow in influence to be effective in any central zone of education

Changing role of art education

One of the problems facing the art educator in a changing society is the need to re-assess constantly his role and the function of his subject.

Previous generations possibly enjoyed a form of stability in which the character of art was more constant and the definition of its nature generally accepted. Today such certainty is not present, and we have a flexible and permissive concept of what constitutes 'art'. The boundaries defining art and beauty are not so clearly marked and our understanding of the meaning of art is constantly being challenged and extended.

In such a context our present responsibilities, as visual educators, are concerned with defining a meaningful and significant role for art education in a rapidly changing mass industrial society. This problem is consistent with the dynamic concept of education. Education cannot be seen as a static unchanging body but rather a process capable of identifying the new and changing needs and of providing experience and activity appropriate to these needs.

This sequence is of course parallel to the universal design process and helps place design education as a central, all-embracing activity.

We are educating people for a world that is changing more rapidly than ever before, as a direct consequence of the technological and scientific revolution. Education must therefore aim at adaptability. We need people who are adaptable, not only in a vocational sense, but also in their social and moral attitudes.

Traditionally 'art' has tended to play a peripheral role, both in society and education. At one extreme we have art as either an activity for the gifted few, or as a cultural 'fringe benefit' for those who have completed the more serious business of education. We have 'Friday afternoon' art appreciation added in an effort to balance a heavily loaded science and technically orientated senior school timetable.

At the other extreme we have art as a therapy, for bored or backward children and adults; a hobby or expressive play, loose in its function but satisfying provided we are all busy. Clearly this is an over-stated picture but nonetheless one which generally reflects the dual peripheral roles of art education.

School timetables further reflect this tendency with heavy over-loading of 'lower' streams in art activity, and the dropping of all art by examination groups around the third year. The subject possibly re-emerges as 'art appreciation' or 'liberal cultural studies', as a minority option in the top form.

We desperately need teachers with a broad view of culture. Creativity in schools is so often found only in the art room or weekly music lesson. The child's world, however, is rich in popular and living culture, so often in conflict with the rigid ideas of adult art. We need to remove tension areas between strict attitudes of what constitutes culture and the existing culture of urban life. Often the teacher is frustrated by the child's rejection of adult cultural values – though the rejection may indicate the narrowness of his own view of culture.

Obviously the considerable value of these peripheral activities should not be denied. The contribution art activity plays as a therapy is respected and the educational value of expressive practical work clearly admitted. Equally no one would dismiss our fine cultural traditions or deny the essential nature of the Arts in society. What is of serious concern is the enormous gap existing between these two areas.

A traditional tendency has always been to consider art as a decoration of life rather than central to it. Alternatively, craft has been considered as purely vocational, without intellectual merit. These separate attitudes have restricted both these areas from contributing to the mainstream of education. However, design education can bring these points together and involves a full range of other subjects.

The need to establish a central role for art education in schools is urgent. Within the schools the major function of design education could be concerned with creating a meaningful, broadly based, central role for visual education.

Both in society and education we have long-established traditions of literacy. Parents are concerned if children cannot read or write, and a general anxiety is shown if these skills are not mastered. We also have numeracy as a major educational foundation, with similar concern if success is not evident. Much importance is placed on these skills but no one parent, child or teacher is over-anxious if the child leaves school totally lacking in visual literacy.

In addition to literacy and numeracy we need a third fundamental language, that of vision. This has sometimes been called 'graphicacy'. Whatever the term, what is clearly evident is the need for visual literacy to complete a balanced educational structure. Visual education has been seriously neglected.

Such an attitude is unfortunately restricting. It may perhaps be helpful to argue that the artist is not a special kind of person at all and that everyone is a special kind of artist. Everyone can write but are not all called 'authors'. Similarly we can all give visual form to materials and our surroundings and communicate in other ways than words without being labelled 'artist'.

Education is concerned with the response we make to our surroundings. Experience, knowledge and understanding can change the nature of our response. An articulate and responsible active response to a designed environment can only be made by a visually articulate population.

Our visual heritage stems from a classical European tradition. Present day industrial mass culture has a unique form and its understanding requires a re-appraisal of our critical yardsticks. Traditionally the literate and articulate middle and upper classes have tended to be the ones responding actively to the decisions of planners and environment makers.

If art is a form of expression and communication we should study in depth how ideas can be expressed and concepts communicated visually. If design is concerned with the function and appearance of the man-made environment, largely three-dimensional, we should have experience of the widest range of structural problems and the materials concerned. If our society is dominated by the products of technology, and the decisions of designers, we should study machine processes, the materials of technology and have experience of how decisions are made.

Visual education in terms of perception, communication, function, structure and appearance, choice and decision making, cannot be experienced solely through drawing and painting. The practical area of study needs to be broad, inter-disciplinary and flexible, extending the frontiers of what we think constitute 'art activities'.

Central to any creative and critical education of vision is the process of problem solving. We need to build personal judgments rather than join a litany to the pressures of fashion, mass media and advertising.

Within education we tend to give solutions and require pupils to remember imposed and established answers. This leaves the young person with no experience of making decisions or of developing his own value judgments. We are inclined to impose judgments for example by 'ticking' when things are 'right' and putting crosses on every other occasion. We do not make much effort to encourage natural problem-solving inventiveness with its inbuilt learning and evaluation processes.

Problem solving is central to art and design activities and to learning and discovery but, more than anything else, it is a fundamental part of everyday life. We make many decisions quite naturally and are in fact acting as designers in solving problems in this way. Much the same basic logical considerations apply to more difficult design problems.

Before locating the learning process within problem solving we must first assume that there is a basic difference between education and training. We would also need to assume that we cannot strictly be taught anything and can only genuinely develop or learn through experience. The ancient maxim, 'I was told and I forgot, I saw and I remembered, I did and I understood', illustrates this point very well. The idea of education through experience is contained precisely within the activity of problem solving.

The three basic stages of problem-solving work have much in common with the processes of both creativity and education.
1   We identify a problem, we observe and isolate, we extend our experience and are made aware of a need. We collect data and information, we measure and quantify.

2 We propose solutions — we examine known solutions, we extend our inventive capacity (creativity) both rationally, by measured logic, or more freely by trial and error.

3 We test and evaluate our solution. We discover if our solution is adequate or inadequate, efficient or inefficient. We build up our judgment values. We find out why our solution was effective or ineffective. Both growth and development occur.

The evaluation stage is critical to learning. We should not embark on any problem solving until we have established the self-contained evaluation criteria inherent in the problem. So frequently after doing something, we are told it is 'nice,' 'good,' or some other vague value judgment is given. It is ticked, marked, exhibited, or assessed. Often the evaluation is external to the child's experience and based on chance, personal taste, or nebulous fashionable ideas of what is good or bad.

Our methods of evaluation must become more accurate. The maximum learning within problem solving occurs at the evaluation stage. It is not sufficient to think we know or to hazard a guess; discovery occurs only when we can actually define and understand the reasons.

Teacher and pupil together must devise ways of analysing and finding out why solutions are appropriate or inappropriate. No problem solving exists unless the criterion for testing is contained in the initial brief.

The discovery processes of why things work and why they look the way they do is the educational essence of problem solving. Creative problem solving without accurate testing machinery is valueless. Our evaluation must be articulate, our proposed solution must

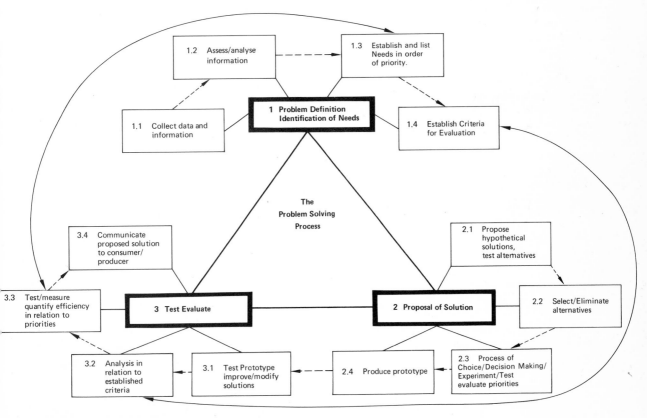

2 The problem solving process. It is important to stress the necessary reference back from Stage 3 to the initial criteria and priorities in Stage 1

be able to be tested effectively and not vaguely considered in terms of 'I think I like it' or 'I think it will work'.

If we have been involved in the identification of a problem and the proposal of solutions we should also be involved in the testing and evaluation of our solutions.

The teacher or external examination system are no longer the only evaluators. The role of the teacher begins to change. The emphasis moves from critic or 'marker' of work to a role of educational designer. Such a person is one who can involve young people in significant and appropriate problems, and set problems involving critical visual issues and human needs. The educational designer requires to discuss and construct the problem-solving brief to ensure that at least two objects are achieved.

1　That relevant experience is gained to meet the needs of the particular group.

2　That self-evaluation of the solution is built into the brief. For example:

A need to understand and experience the basic principles of structure with a particular material. A problem is therefore given to 'build a structure to support a given weight'. This is obviously very loose but if we add, 'build a structure to hold a given weight using a minimum amount of material', we add a further element of constraint. This constraint although a very crude example, does two things.

1　It extends our creative frontiers. (To solve the problem we must exercise more creative inventiveness.)

2　It gives a criterion for evaluation.

The most efficient or appropriate solution will not just be the one that supports the weight — but the structure that achieves this with the minimum use of material.

Although a simple example it shows that by structuring the problem-solving brief we can, as a natural corollary, stimulate inventive thinking and use of materials and at the same time, build in a criterion for testing and measuring.

Decision-making experience is a fundamental part of education but more than anything else should be central to any 'creative' subjects. We need such experience if we are going to make any sense of the decisions imposed on us in a designed, man-made technology, or make any judgments ourselves.

Creativity by its very nature is concerned with decision making. Too much so-called art is a kind of play, or 'apparent' creativity, which does not equip the young person to make critical personal decisions free from external pressures.

We mistakenly equate creativity with drawing and painting and other established activities of the art room. All too often what is produced is a stereotyped pastiche of what we think child art should look like.

Creative thinking, discovery and critical personal decision making should not be restricted to art.

Educational creativity (especially in the middle grades) should not be added as a liberalising factor in small doses of art at off-peak learning times. Problem-solving creativity can be present in decision making which is related to design education in all subjects.

3　The involvement with other disciplines that design activity naturally promotes

The Revolving Inter-relationships between the Design Process and Other Areas of Study

The Design Process as a Vehicle for Learning

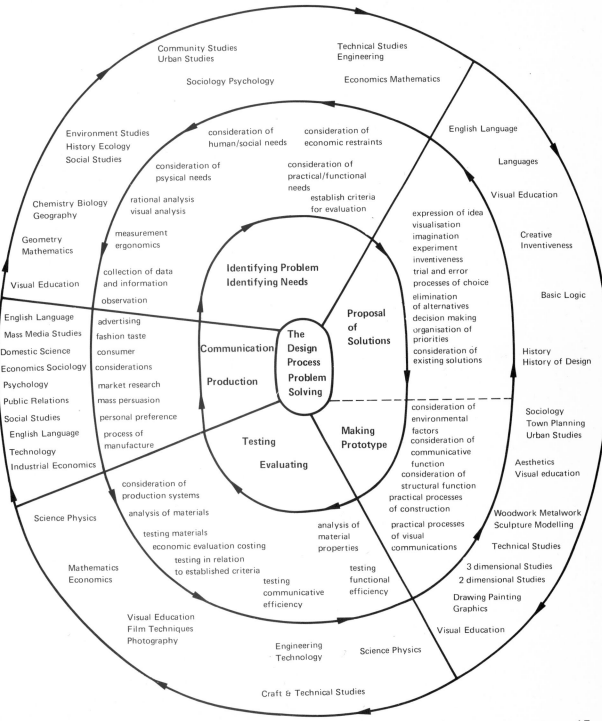

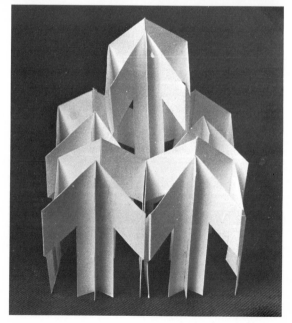

4, 5, 6 Structural problem. Given the shape of one unit this has to be developed into a three-dimensional and two-dimensional structure. No adhesives to be used. The solutions illustrate how the ultimate shape owes its visual character to the initial unit

Practical work

Part 2

Structure and physical function

Identifying the visual determinants of the appearance of objects surrounding us is crucial to visual education (see figure 79). This should not be the sole responsibility of the art educator, in fact such a narrow outlook would be as unrepresentative as is much of the present emphasis on 'expressive free creativity'. In addition to the traditional creative scope presented in art rooms we need to study much broader spheres. The object must be to present young people with the widest potential for visual study.

As a central activity, studying why things look the way they do seems to offer beginnings for visual study.

We can, of course, study the appearance and structure of objects when we draw them. The tendency however is to record the 'outer' appearance without understanding the underlying reasons. It takes a very skilled and mature observer to understand, through drawing alone, the structural reasons for any particular form. It is important to realise that visual study can take many forms in addition to drawing. For example, we are studying visually if we identify the structural function which an observed object is performing, and then construct in another material a different structure to do the same thing. We learn in a practical way how forms are arrived at and what physical changes materials can undergo.

There are in fact many ways of studying visually, and practical problem solving is just another way of understanding the structural appearance of the world.

So much of the man-made world is three dimensional that we need to have experience of structural problems, and to explore the properties of materials. The man-made and natural objects around us all have different qualities; some are rigid and heavy, others flimsy and light, some hard and brittle while others are flexible. All these varying factors depend on the materials used, the processes that have formed them, and the jobs they have to do.

There are many reasons why things look as they do – structural and communicative factors, processes of manufacture, economics, marketing, social requirements – all in varying degrees of importance. This particular section separates physical function and material properties from other determinates.

Materials can perform many functions and part of the designer's job is to extend his practical vocabulary in understanding their wide potential. Similarly, in the classroom it seems appropriate to use the widest range of materials possible in solving structural problems to give experience of their widely varying qualities.

Materials have to hold weight, contain objects, span space, enclose areas, obtain height. The problem areas are therefore basic but the potential materials for such jobs are many. Technology and science have produced whole ranges of new materials. Many of these new materials do not have a craft tradition and are often available as industrial or domestic discards, having considerable educational potential. We are not limited by traditional methods of use, and we have to discover for ourselves how to manipulate such new materials.

Many of the problems in this section are therefore about basic structural functions. Solutions have, however, been encouraged in a wide range of materials and we begin to understand why things look the way they do.

Work related to structural factors that affect appearance, is a study area that can have its origins in the art room or 'visual education workshop'. It is by its very nature interdisciplinary. Obviously such work may frequently include aspects of mathematics and simple science and in this way the frontiers and experience of art are extended. Art is not a narrow specialist activity and as soon as we endeavour to study such factors as structural influences on form we reach into a more central area touching engineering, technical studies and mathematics.

The proliferation of technology, new sciences, new manufacturing processes and new social economic conditions make it impossible for any one designer to work in isolation covering all these specialist requirements, unlike the craftsman in pre-industrial society. More and more, he has to work as part of a team of specialists or in close relation to other experts.

The importance of design spreading 'naturally' into other activities is critical. The artificial segregation of subjects can be educationally negative, but equally the artificial 'getting together' inherent in some inter-disciplinary work can also be meaningless.

The real value occurs when we encounter another discipline as a natural part of our problem-solving activity.

We do not realise we are doing 'mathematics' or 'science' – we are fundamentally concerned with solving a problem and are not conscious of restricting subject labels which frighten us, and inhibit learning – and yet we engage all manner of disciplines as part of the activity. This non-selfconscious involvement with other disciplines is a natural by-product of problem-solving activity.

The inter-disciplinary nature of design education and problem-solving activity obviously poses questions about the role of a single subject enclosed classroom and of the single specialist teacher operating in isolation. This problem is referred to in more depth in the final section of the book. However, it clearly emerges as a matter for consideration as soon as we become involved in any practical design problem solving.

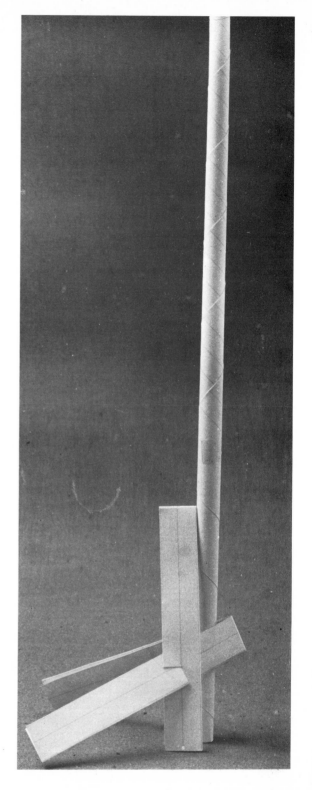

7 *Solution to the problem of building the highest self-supporting structure from one piece of thin paper. The folded base support permits the long cylinder of rolled paper to stand firmly*

18

above
8 *Problem-solving game. Group members are given a standard amount of material and have to place a given weight at the farthest distance from a fixed point. An activity giving experience of the quality of materials and the visual forms produced in solving a standard structural problem*

9 *Weight-holding structural problem. Build a structure, spanning two points, to hold maximum weight while using minimum material. The established restraints give a logical basis for evaluation. The solution can be evaluated according to easily measured factors: the amount of weight held and the quantity of material used*

19

right
10 Space enclosing – another standard function of material structures. Problem: to enclose a given area without internal support. The interlocking units operate without adhesives

below
11 A further solution to the problem of space enclosing, involving a considerable link with the study of geometry and mathematics

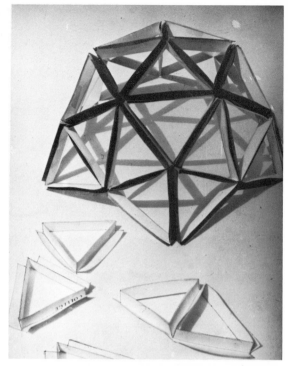

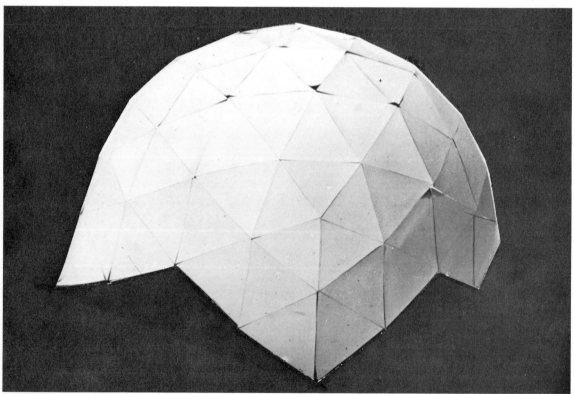

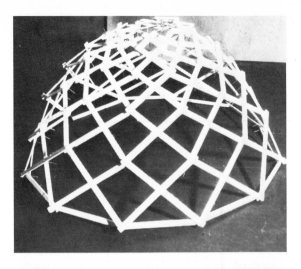

12 to 15 A space-enclosing problem related to a project with local schools. The identified problem was to provide a quiet, portable, space enclosure for infants in crowded open-planned areas. Students and older children were involved in this design project. The work offered opportunity for practical work of some educational/social purpose and helped establish new working relationships between older pupils, working for the very young, and between students and teachers

12, 13, 14 Initial exploratory exercises with materials. Exploring alternative potential solutions of joining units, lattice-folding strips and forms that emerge naturally from folding paper and giving the material some structural strength

15 One of the finished cardboard prototypes for this project

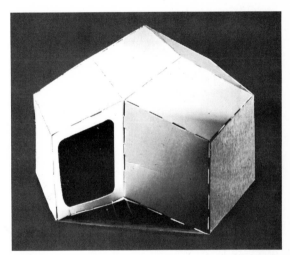

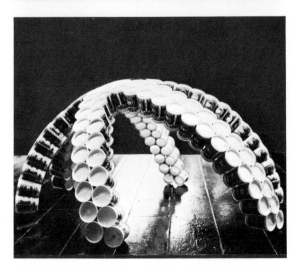

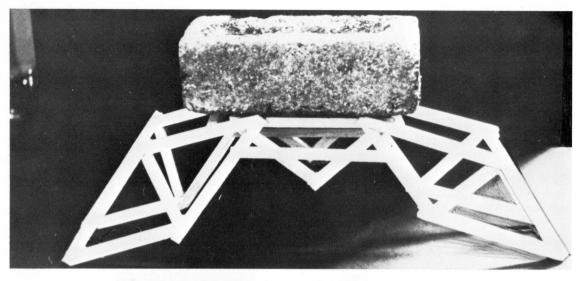

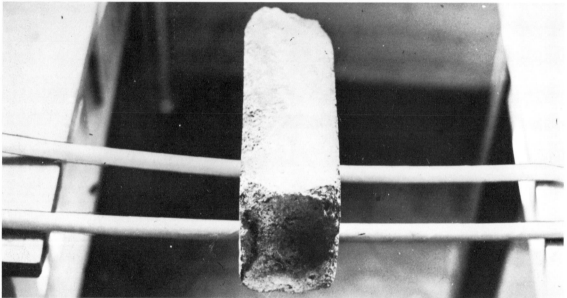

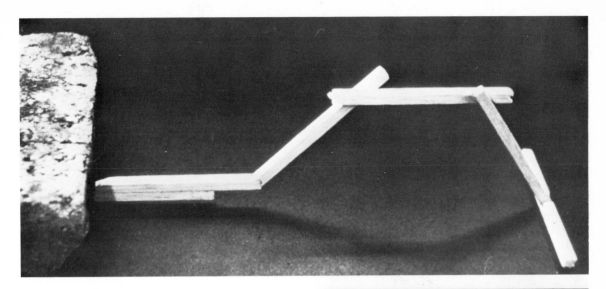

16 to 19   *Different solutions to the same structural problem: to span a given space while supporting the weight of one brick*
18, 19   *Solutions which in essence have 'beaten' the design brief. The brick is supported and the space spanned, though the unexpected has revealed another learning point related to the idea of cantilever. This illustrates the need to define and discuss all problem definitions very thoroughly with the group. In fact a collective discussion of the wording and objectives of the brief is an essential educational aspect of problem-solving work*

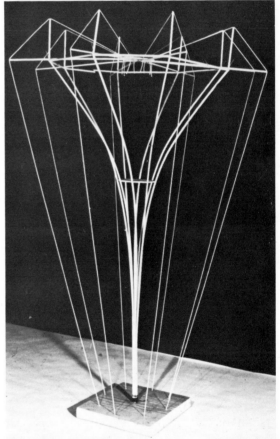

20   *A further solution to the problem of building the highest self-supporting structure from the minimum material*

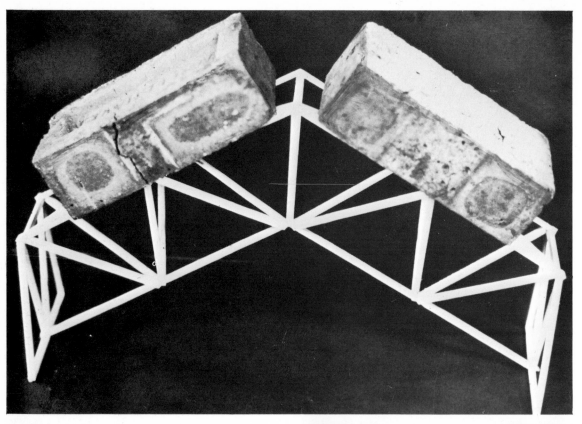

21, 22 *Problem: to design a structure to hold the maximum weight using the minimum number of identical structural units (drinking straws)*

above
23, 24   Practical problem solving related to the idea of simple mechanical movement
23   A structure to combine simultaneously two different directional movements
24   A solution to the problem of transferring movement from one plane to another

left
25   Part of an interdisciplinary group project concerned with devising a mechanism (from all manner of discarded materials) which could transfer the minimum source power to the maximum movement energy. The 'source power' was an elastic band, a dropping marble, a dripping tap and a burning candle. This project, although centred around art work, involved many other disciplines. Mechanical operations play a considerable part in the appearance of the man-made world and this appears a particularly relevant visual design problem

below left
26   A solution to the problem of constructing a self-propelling form capable of maintaining motion, on a level surface, for the maximum period of time

27 A simple problem-solving exercise to assemble a selection of discarded materials and construct from them a form which can be totally articulated

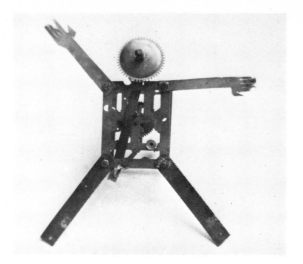

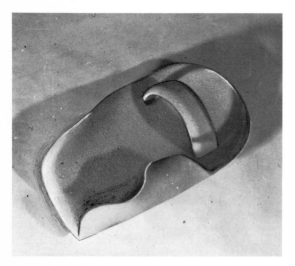

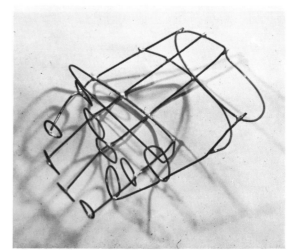

28, 29, 30 Simple problem-solving exercises in hand-held ergonomics

above

28, 29 Problems concerned with construction of 'glove form'. Moulded polyethylene foam and brazed wire. Both problems required thorough visual analysis and measurement of the hand (crucial information collecting aspects of the design process). The amount of 'looking' at the hand and documentation, in ways other than traditional life-drawing observation, was a useful by-product of this project

right

30 Problem: to design a hand held device to operate finger controls with comfort and minimum wrist movement. These are simple 'sculptural' design problems giving some initial experience of the important relationship between objects and the human scale

31   *The Ergonomic Chair. A design project sub-mitted as part of study for the first A Level Design Paper (Oxford Examination Delegacy 1971)*

A series of rods allow for variations of body size to be considered in determining the form of the seat. The project set out to design a device which could be rapidly adjusted to accommodate varying sitting positions

32 Part of a project to design a safety play car. Ergonomic jig to collect data on varying measurements, of a wide age range of young children. The jig was placed in a number of junior schools and the information was collected and collated by the children as part of their school work

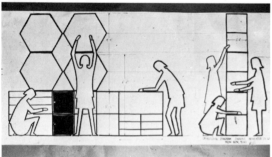

33, 34 Part of a project to design simple multipurpose furniture for the art room to accommodate display, storage and working surfaces
33 The relationship of structures to compromise standard heights of various age groups of pupils

34 Prototype models. Such projects, related to educational needs and problems, develop after earlier experience of simple basic problem solving work. Teenage pupils, teacher-training students and teachers work together on such projects. The design process naturally accommodates different skills and offers opportunity for varying individual responsibilities

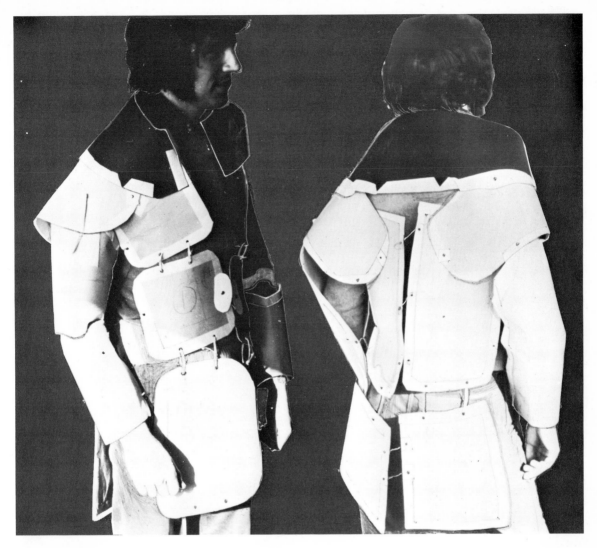

35 The design process and human measurement. 'Dress design' as moving three-dimensional structure. The problem set was to design a 'garment' to fit all group members, which would allow certain physical movements to be made without the garment splitting.

The main aim was to experience the problem of mass design for different sizes of people and how we have to arrive at 'compromise' measurements to accommodate varying human sizes. The analysis and collection of data was a critical aspect. The project also aimed to illustrate the idea that dress design is not just about 'fashion and style' but is also concerned with principles of construction and is potentially part of three-dimensional design study. This project was very much a 'game activity' involving an all male group

36 Container design problem. Simple problem to contain a given number of glasses securely in a package, using cardboard and paper. A problem again related to the significance of measurement. The form of the container being determined not only by the material used but by the dimensions of the glass

37–40 Hand-held objects, problem-solving study. Thirteen-year-old pupils redesigning hand grips to replace broken handles on tools and domestic science utensils in the school.

The initial stage of the project was to determine the most efficient size and form of grip to fit widely varying hand sizes

37 Plasticine *moulded to fit the hand efficiently*

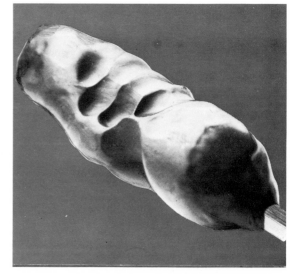

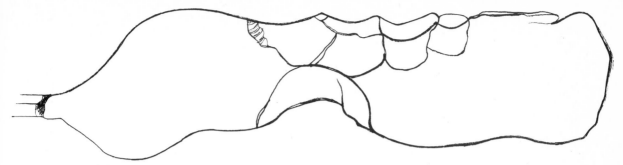

38 *Drawing of moulded form*

39 Plasticine *on saucepan*

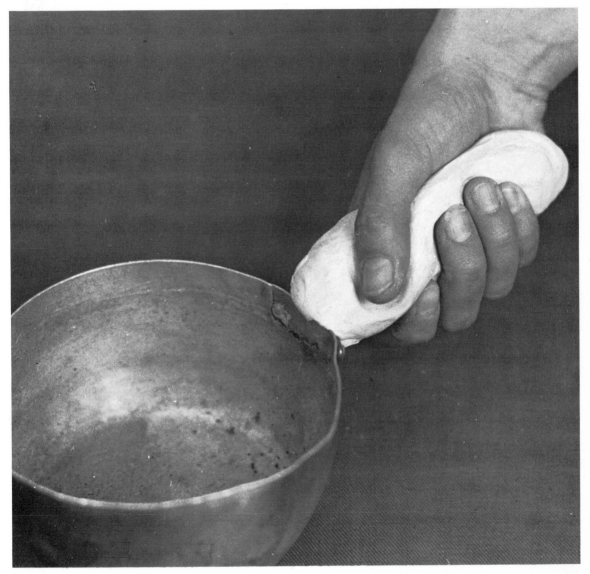

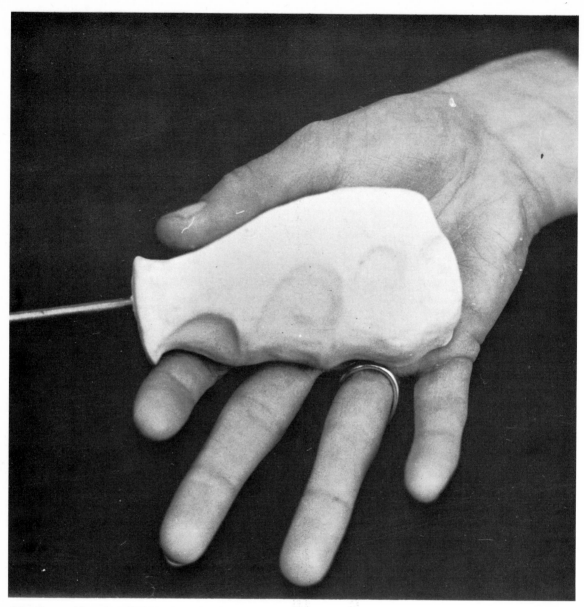

40   *Screwdriver handle being modelled*

The soft forms were 'gripped' by selected age/size range of users to modify form for collective use
*   A useful example not only of a realistic design problem, but of inventive design methodology being employed to collect information easily and efficiently*

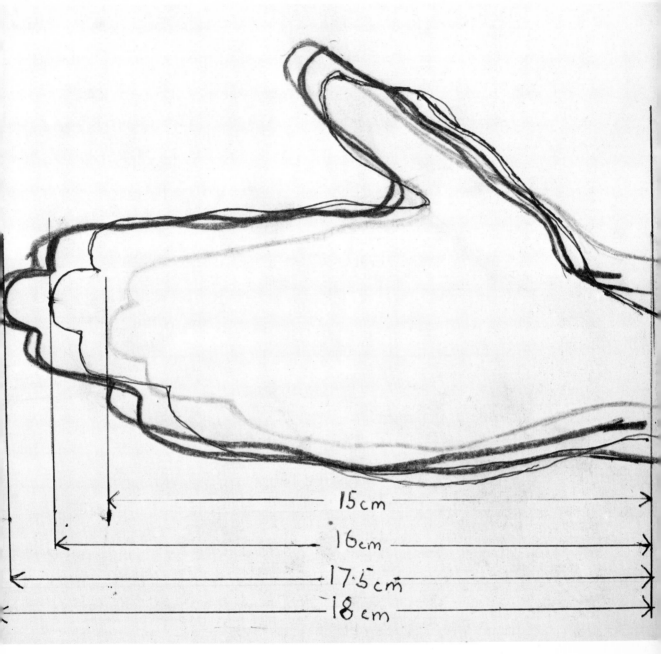

15 cm

16 cm

17·5 cm

18 cm

above and pp. 34, 35
41   Ten-year-old children — study of varying hand measurements within a group. Basic study of design problem for the design of any hand-held or hand-operated device for varying hand sizes. Simple experience in 'ergonomics' and in collecting, collating and presenting information, which is a basic factor in decision making and the design process

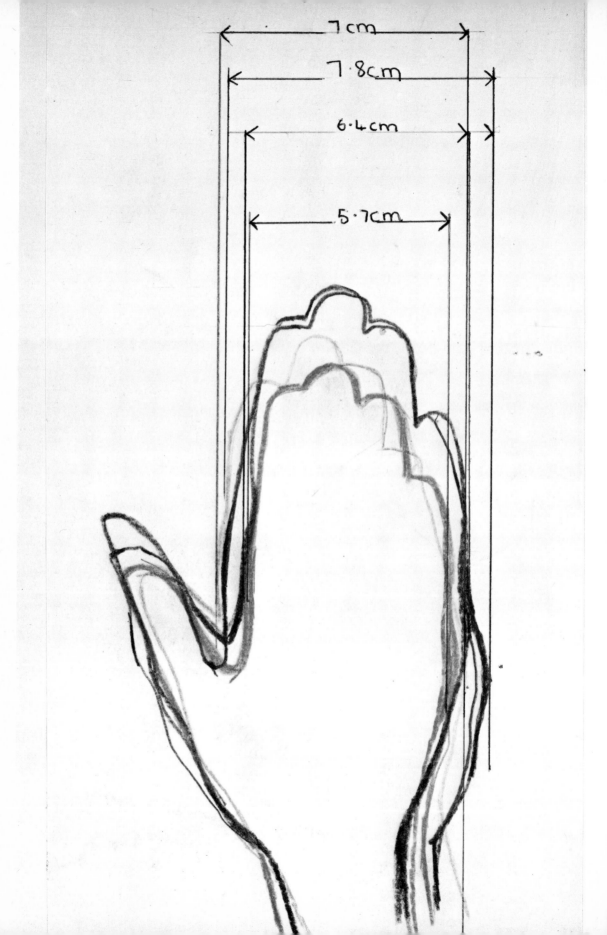

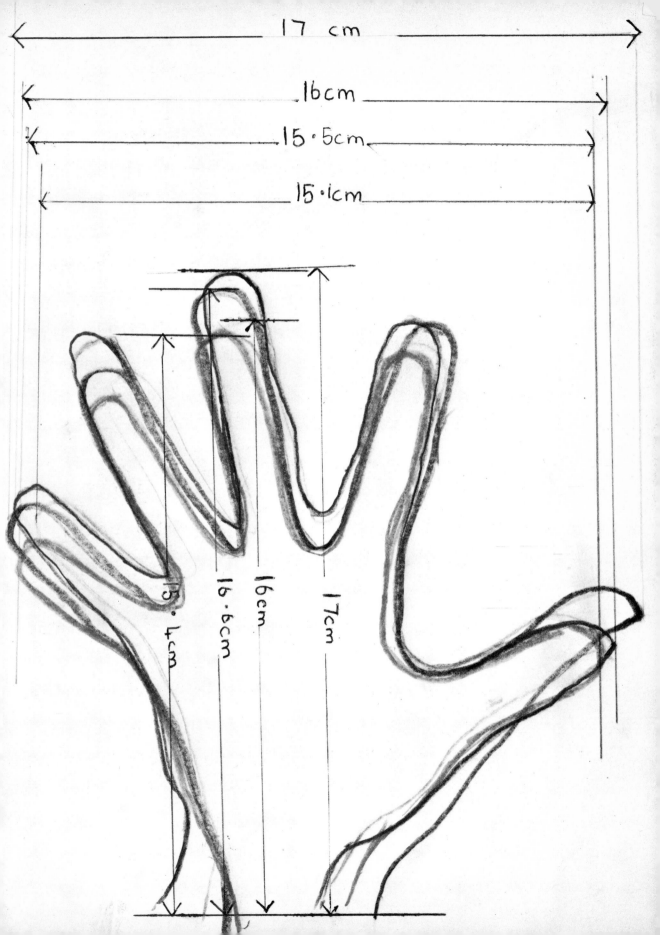

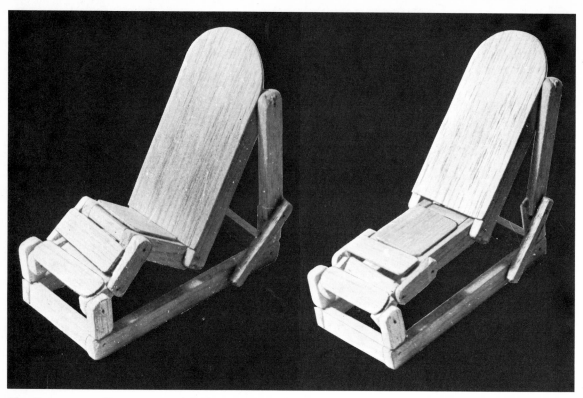

42 Teenage pupil's prototype model for an adjust-
able seating device

right
43 Analytical drawings by children studying
ergonomic considerations of classroom seating. The
project included studying problems of mass seating
and devising methods of studying the varying
dimensions of members of the class. A moveable
card template of a seated figure was made and
drawn round in all sitting positions with actual
measurements then added

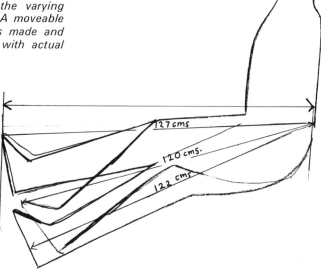

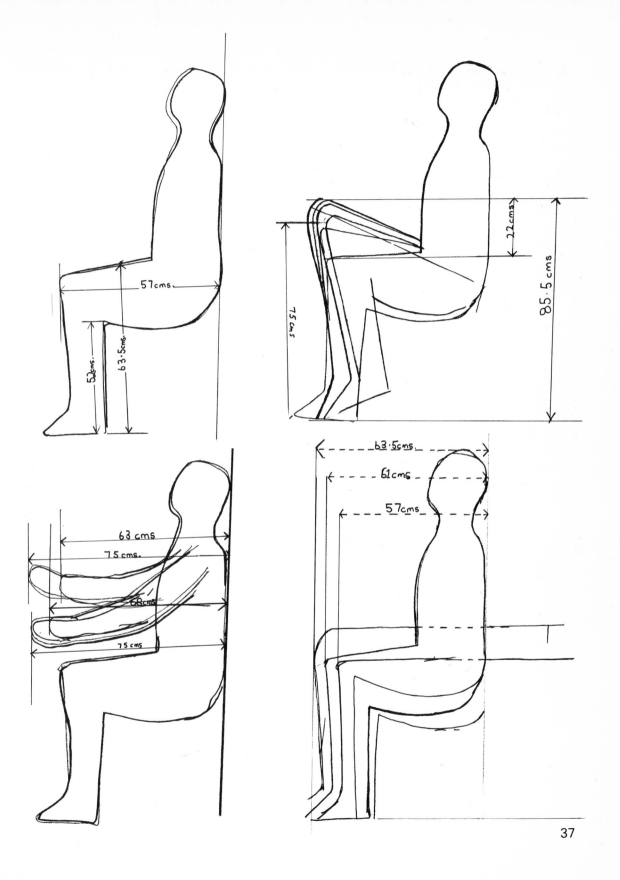

57cms.

52cms.

63.5cms.

75cms

22cms

85.5 cms

63cms

75cms.

68cms

75cms

63.5cms.

61cms.

57cms.

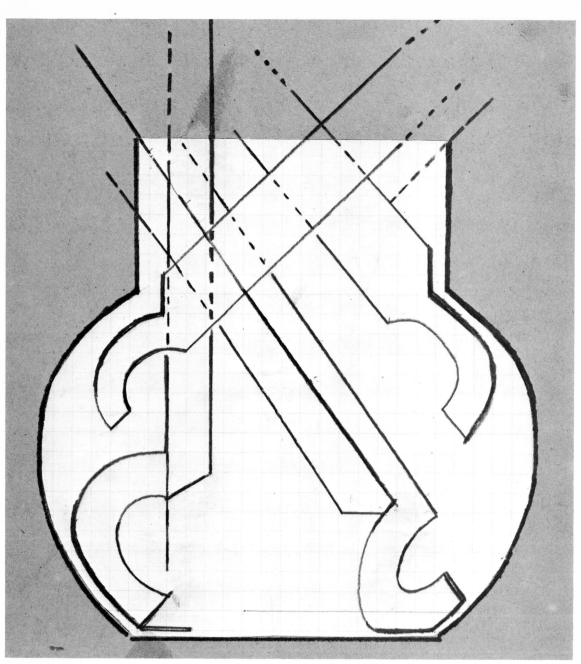

44, 45, 46 School project studying how operational function and dimensional restraints determine form. Problem: to design an implement capable of removing all the contents from a given container

above
44 One of many initial drawings to determine interior form of container and what two-dimensional shape would fit the form

45, 46 *Cardboard prototypes with container. The project potentially linked art and technical drawing and included a strong 'game' factor, together with a discovery of some of the measurable factors that determine the form of objects. Elements of economics and waste factors were also discussed*

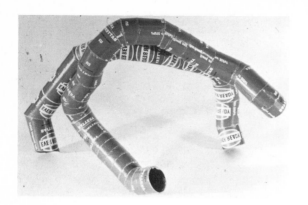

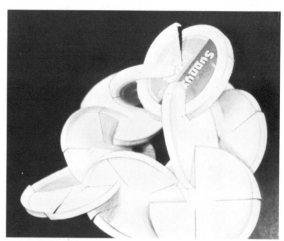

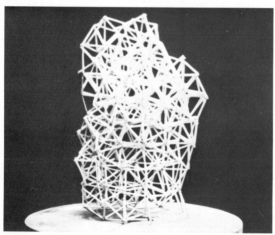

47 to 52 Examples of different solutions to the same problem. The initial problem was to design a structure capable of being extended in more than one direction. Given a series of identical units the object was to explore joining methods necessary for the development of multi-directional structures

opposite
53 Unit structure. Problem: to design a single unit that when joined together can be extended in more than one direction

40

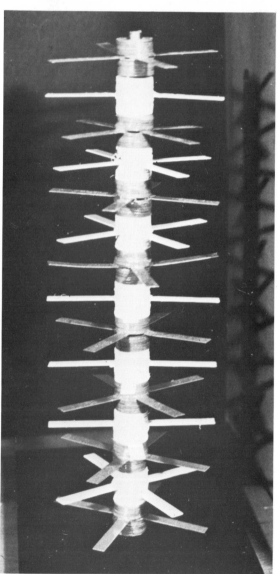

top
54, 55   Geometric unit structures

above and right
56, 57   Unit structure using discarded industrial products. One of the inherent potentials of industrial waste is the availability of identical mass-produced units. Such units are ideal for the study of a three-dimensional unit structure
56   Electrical transformer units providing an abundance of units
57   Tower made from mechanical units

58 Ceramic unit structure. Part of a project building forms from three basic units. The final form emerges as a natural 'organic' result of the units used

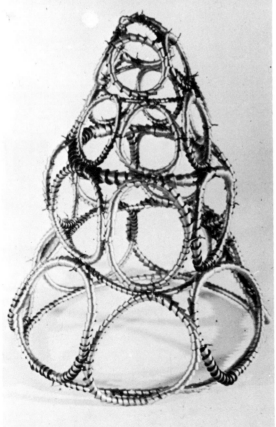

59 Lathe-turning waste used as part of a problem to construct a form from waste units of the same character

60 *Unit structure using thin plastic sheet*

61 Unit structure using thin card. The aim was not to make an 'art object' but to study the intrinsic nature of unit growth and visual order. Given a number of identical units the form emerges naturally from the visual character of the individual units as they are constructed in an ordered way

45

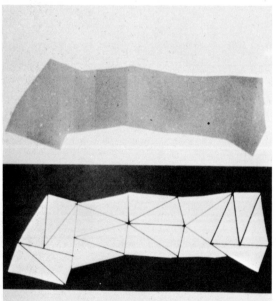

62   Moveable unit structure from scrap mechanical units, pop riveting joints. Small hand pop riveter used, suitable for standard art room work

left
63   Unit structure in two-dimensions. Problem: to construct a two-dimensional shape from a given number of identical units. The units must fit together without any space in between to form the larger shape. The problem is then for someone else to identify the visual character of the initial unit from which the shape is built up. The aim is to experience how the character of a shape or form reflects the basic unit from which it 'grows'. If an odd number of units is used it is more difficult to disguise the character of the smaller unit. The illustration gives the total shape and diagram shows how it is made up of identical units

opposite and pp. 48, 49 and 50
64 to 67   Unit structure in two-dimensions. Further solutions to this problem, showing the initial unit and the relationship the larger shape, made up of these units, has to it

49

68 Basic stencil printing, visual exercise. One given basic unit has to be printed in sequence, each unit touching. The progression must touch all four sides of a given rectangle

below
69 Two-dimensional unit patterns. Basic printing exercise using the ends of pencils, cylinders, screw heads, folded card, etc. The object of this study is to examine how patterns and forms can develop naturally from the ordered repetition of units

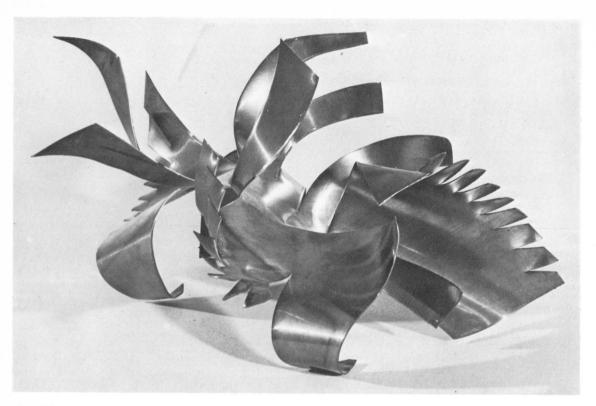

above
70 Exploration of a simple process and the quality of a material. Exercise in cutting (metal shears). Problem to transfer a flat piece of thin tin to a three-dimensional volume without waste

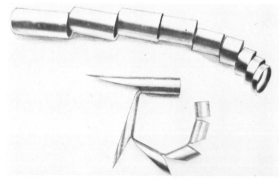

right
71, 72 Exploring potential of process of cutting (hack saw) with scrap pipe and metal extrusion. Problem: To change a rigid straight piece of metal into a three-dimensional form with the use of saw cuts only.

All these basic exercises with scrap materials introduce young pupils to the potential of hand tool processes, the quality of materials and how visual form can emerge as a result of such activity. This work was introduced into the 'art' room helping to link work with other technical study areas

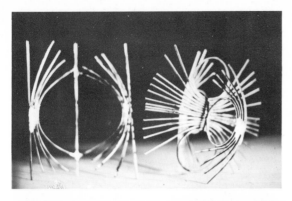

73 Structural problem of measurement, joining and unit structure. Identical short lengths of straight wire are bent in a measured equal progression from a straight line to a semi-circle. Having produced these units they are then brazed together and the final form grows 'automatically' from the prepared units. A visual study problem combining technical drawing, art and design studies

74 Experiment in vacuum forming plastic. Art/design workshop project to build a vacuum former. Domestic vacuum cleaner to remove air from screwed down, air-tight box, in which plastic sheet is placed over former. The sheet is heated over an electric ring

below
75 Vacuum formed pencil holder. Showing finished form and wood mould over which plastic is formed. Such projects seem particularly relevant as plastics begin to dominate the man-made product market.

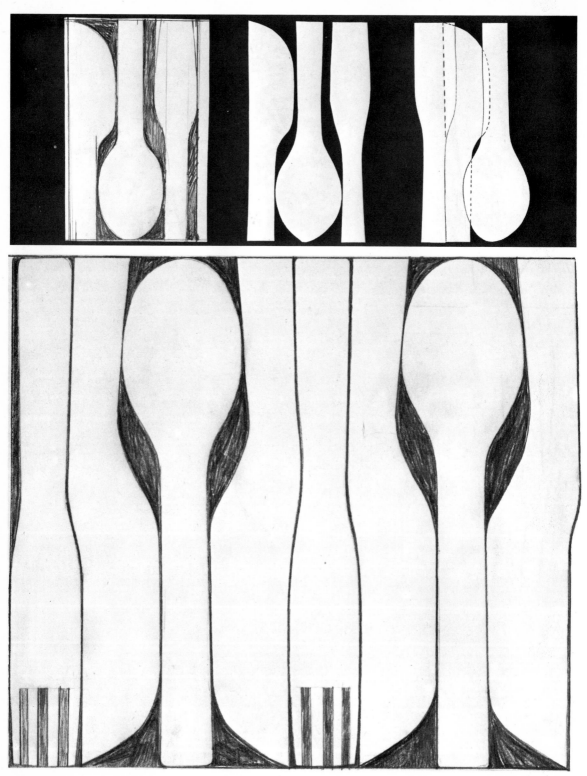

54

opposite
76 Practical design problem identifying one of the factors (economy of material and production) that may influence the appearance of an object. Problem: To design disposable cutlery for air-line meals. Specific consideration given to the economy of material and need to get maximum number cut from given rectangle of material. Drawings show how the form develops and alters as consideration of achieving minimum waste develop

77, 78 Design education in relation to local community. Examples of students' work with local school for physically handicapped girls

above
77 Play equipment project. Plastic tubes and nylon rope used to construct a multi-level caterpillar for traversing rough open area. Projects of this kind are logical developments of earlier study of problem solving and design methods. The work involves students, not only in practical design study, but also in educational, social and human problems

left
78 Glassfibre sphere. A safety rocking toy, part of a student programme designing play equipment for handicapped children.

A large rubber tyre tube used as a buffer and a glassfibre sphere for a 'cockpit' in which the passenger sits. However violently the device is rocked it is impossible for it to be over-turned

55

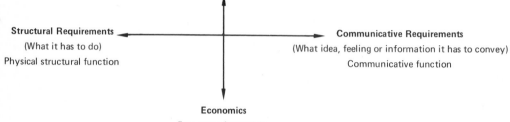

The Determinants of Visual Form

The factors that determine why an object looks the way it does

The order of priority varies with each object

Processes of Forming

Intrinsic nature of materials

machine / industrial / hand / organic

Structural Requirements

(What it has to do)

Physical structural function

Communicative Requirements

(What idea, feeling or information it has to convey)

Communicative function

Economics

Economy of materials

Economy of labour / Economy of time

Minimum wastage from raw material

Economy of production method and structural processes

Economy of storage / packing / transport

Projected Price of Product

Size — Operational Ergonomics

Human scale / Users' measurements

human movement

Transporting / storage / packing / weight

environmental scale

Consumer Requirements

Consumer / User Needs

Specific Market Destination

Social Class Group

Age / Sex Group

Income Group

Intended duration of Product

(short term / permanent / disposable)

Operational Location

(where it is going to be used)

specific market appeal considerations

79   *All the problem-solving activities in this section, on structural function, and the next on communicative function, are concerned fundamentally with understanding why things appear as they do. This chart shows the interaction of factors determining visual form*

Visual communication

It is possibly easier to recognise the reasons why things look as they do when thinking of aspects of physical function. We can all understand that a chair, for instance, has certain visual characteristics determined by its function of holding human weight off the ground and supporting a form that can be measured and weighed. Such aspects of function are directly obvious and simply quantifiable. But structural function, the nature of materials and the measurement of human scale, is only one part of the determining elements of visual form.

The same chair has other equally important functions in communicating for example what type of chair it is; whether it is for important occasions or is a modest everyday affair, for fast jet set people or quiet elderly folk.

Visual form can tell us many important things and the communicative function of an object is equally as important as the structural function. We do however tend to overlook this aspect of function and think it applies only to practical physical factors.

This section is specifically concerned with exploring aspects of visual function and trying to discover, through appropriate problem-solving activities, why things look the way they do.

The balance of the various determinates of visual form varies from object to object.

Sometimes structural function or operational efficiency dominate while at other times, or with other objects, communicative factors are more important. The order of priorities varies depending on the total job any object has to perform.

In any visual design study we may be anxious to find out why things look similar or different, trying as part of our educational process to discover more clearly the reasons for the appearance of our surroundings.

In the first section we separated material function from other factors and in this section we isolate the purely visual factor.

More and more information and ideas are given to us in visual form. We see an increasing number of signs, symbols, advertisements, magazines, packages and we visually consume large quantities of film and television. But these are not the only visual things. All the forms of the 'designed' world around us have visual substance and communicate ideas to us, at different levels. Understanding the reasons for these forms is crucial to the development of work in design education.

There are obviously many ways of communicating other than by the written word. Shapes, forms, colours and lines can all give definite ideas or transmit information quickly and clearly. Recognising this fundamental everyday function of visual form is essential for any critical, conscious and visual understanding of our surroundings. Forms, buildings, shapes, objects, colours and pattern all tell us something; either about their function, or owner, or give some other information — they are the way they are for a particular reason.

Churches look different from banks, and sports cars from family saloons, for reasons other than their structural differences; the list is endless and we must extend the areas of visual study in an endeavour to understand the precise reasons for these communicative differences.

There are many elements, found in all kinds of objects and buildings, which are not accounted for by purely structural functional requirements. They are added after problems of material utility and operational efficiency have been solved and are concerned with appearance, communication and human response and reaction to visual form.

In all areas of our environment we communicate precise ideas through the appearance of objects and it is this function of communication that designers, architects and advertisers use as elements determining much of our man-made surroundings.

There are at least two main aspects of visual communication to be considered.

One is that area of visual communication concerned with giving instructions and information and the other is about the communicating of ideas and feelings or the stimulating of reactions. Studying problems in these two fields helps us begin to see the function of mark making and drawing as thinking functions not just as something 'cute' or 'pretty'. In this context drawing and visual communication give us information and perform a precise function.

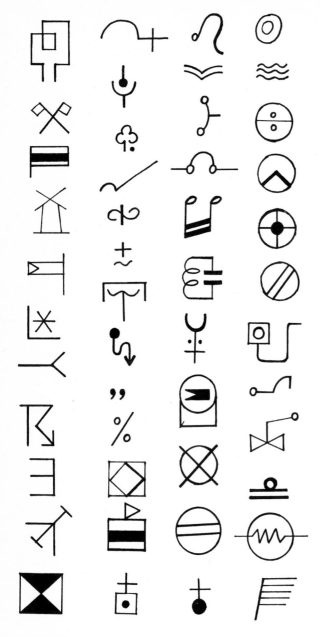

80 *Visual language in action. A selection of visual signs from such widely ranging fields as cartography, chemistry, mathematics, geometry, astronomy, music, engineering, heraldry, shorthand and telecommunications. Also included are railway and traffic signs, military signals and symbols, navigational signs, road signs and some examples from the international language of 'tramps'*

From Shepherd's Glossary of Graphic Signs and Symbols, *Dent*

58

We have a long tradition of sign and symbol in which information has been conveyed visually. This is especially seen in areas where verbal/written language would be inappropriate or inadequate, where speed of reading is critical or where language barriers have to be overcome. Such areas are of course increasing in a mass industrial society — we travel faster, further and more frequently, traffic requires new visual controls. We operate in an international world and require universal languages. Science and technology proliferate and we require coherent diagrams and signs so that we can operate equipment. The organisation of our complex urban movements requires sophisticated yet easily understood visual instructions.

Powerful visual techniques are needed to help sell the increasing number of products of industrial society, in competition for our money and time. We therefore find that buying and choosing is conditioned and influenced by visual impact of advertisements, packaging and display.

Yet the written word has developed total authority in our civilisation. Our cultural traditions are dominated by concepts of literacy and our society is utterly dependent on written values.

Many people think that this puts a restricting influence on our patterns of thought and reaction. We develop our thoughts in straight lines as we read and write, but if we are to come to terms with an electronic age we may need to understand information in new patterns from 'non-linear' sources. We must therefore accept that visual sense impressions are as valid a part of language as any traditional intellectual literacy. Historically, some apparently 'less sophisticated' societies, with highly developed visual form languages, are often more visually aware than traditionally literate societies. However, visual communication study is not limited merely to the communication of information.

The second area referred to is concerned with the communication of concepts and ideas in a non-verbal form. Such non-verbal visual communication is not only seen in design activity but is of course a factor in everyday behaviour. We daily communicate ideas and reactions by gesture, and physical and facial movement. Much of such communication depends on cultural traditions and backgrounds. The designer has to try to overcome these problems, and recognise universal factors of visual language.

Initially we may think that communicating concepts or ideas is less precise or definable in vision than transmitting simple information in this way. However, developing this visual sensitivity is part of any education of the eye and we can ask 'what sort of colour conveys this idea' or 'what shape might appropriately represent or correspond to this sound'. Such questions begin to show the potential communicative content of any form. A complex environment of colour, texture, shape, line and form communicate endless impressions and reactions.

Any critical response to environment is clearly dependent on understanding this language and we need wide experience in problems concerned with the visual communication of ideas and information.

It may help to consider designers in this field not as 'artists' temporarily away from the studio but rather as skilled visual scientists, setting out to communicate well-defined ideas, concepts or even propaganda.

Equally we need to identify the many areas in which visual communication operates, not only immediately obvious graphic design areas but all manner of communicative marks and forms, from the visual form of buildings to the communicative function of dress, from advertisements to signs, double yellow lines, football pitch markings, traffic lights, and navigational buoys. All are giving information and solving basic problems of communication without using words.

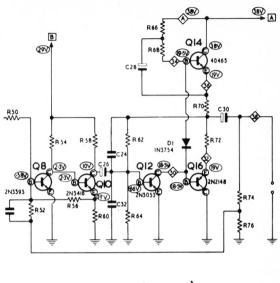

$$x^2 = \sum \frac{(0-E)^2}{E}$$

$$(\overline{x}_1 - \overline{x}_2) = \sqrt{S^2 \left[\frac{n_1 + n_2}{n_1 \times n_2} \right]}$$

81   Drawing used to convey information and ideas. Electrical circuit diagram and mathematical equation. Drawing is not just making pictures and scenes but is a language of communication and expression. We 'express' or show the mathematical problem in a visual form.

This can be well illustrated by the story of the eight year old girl who when asked to 'do some drawing' produced 'four pictures of people and two sums'. She had not yet reached the illogical stage of separating drawing into a different pocket to do with 'art' and equally enjoyed 'drawing' a sum

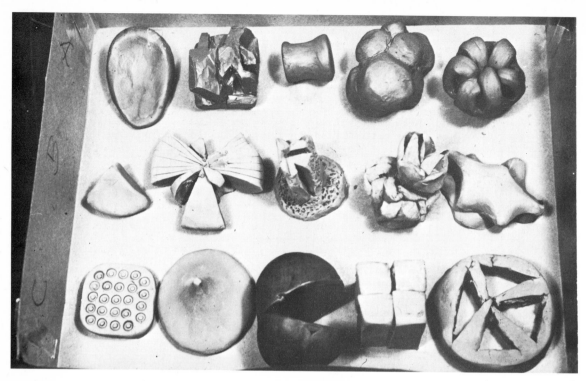

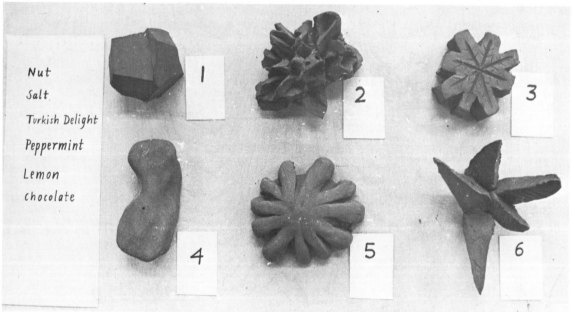

Nut

Salt

Turkish Delight

Peppermint

Lemon

chocolate

82–83 'Chocolate Box' game. Problem: to model (Plasticine or clay) forms to communicate particular flavours. Solutions are then tested for efficiency by another group guessing which flavour each numbered form represents.

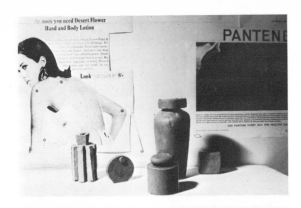

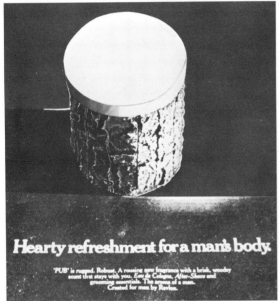

84, 85 *Problem-solving three-dimensional game. Each person is given an advertisement for a container (perfume, soap powder, dog food, etc), but the picture of the container is removed. The problem is to model a form which communicates the idea of the contents, working from the remaining information in the advertisement. Modelled solutions can be evaluated by other group members assessing which model corresponds to which particular advertisement. For this exercise functional factors are separated from communicative considerations. This draws attention to the way in which the idea the container conveys can influence the form as much as whether it holds the contents adequately, pours efficiently and is constructed economically*

86 *Three-dimensional communicative function. Problem set to model a form which would communicate the idea of a particular flavour (eg salt, sugar, pepper). The object to understand that three-dimensional form, in addition to having a structural function, can also be used to convey ideas.*

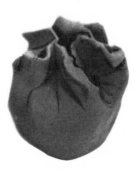

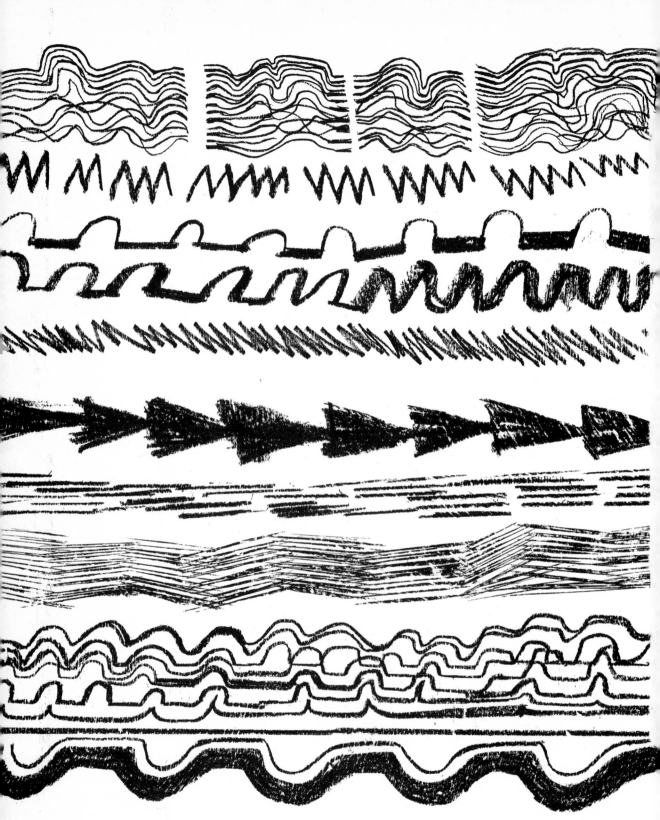

opposite

87 Sound-Vision game. A series of surfaces are 'played' by running a ruler or stick over them. The varying vibrating noises are recorded in lines of 'writing', trying to find the most appropriate line and colour to correspond to each sound. The 'drawing' can be 'tested' by being 'read back' aloud by another person. This work with young children begins to illustrate the communicative function of drawing, that it is not just to do with a picture or 'scene'. We have to start thinking which precise type of line may correspond to a particular sound and discover other functions for visual marks. Links with the language of music and simple concepts of sound waves are immediately obvious integrating factors

88 A further example showing visual equivalents to particular sounds. In these examples tape recorders have been used and considerations of timing and measurement introduced in an attempt to relate the work more closely to music and the study of sound. Also explored were possible ways of 'scoring' visually for art room designed percussion instruments

89 Given a particular cross section, the problem is to translate this into a flat plane using only one visual element (eg line, colour, dot). The solution can be 'tested' by another pupil trying to return the plan to a cross section

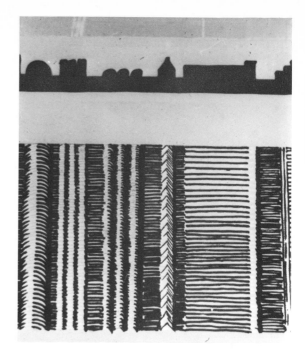

90 Translating a given cross-section to a flat plane, using tone

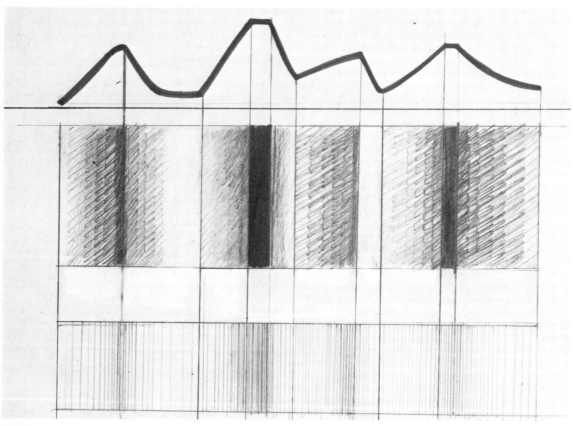

FAST

GAY

FAT

SOFT

SHARP

91 Association of colour with corresponding shape. Pieces of coloured paper, with a white underside, are cut to the shape suggested by the particular colour. The cut out shapes are pasted colour side down onto black paper. The experiment is then tested to assess which shape represents which colour.

This particular example moves from red, in the top left, down in a column approximately through the oranges to bright yellow at the top right, dropping down on the right side through various greens to a circle representing blue

92 The communicative link between an idea and a form. Simple exercises in lettering, designing a letter form to correspond to the idea of the word

overleaf
93 Visual communication chart. Given a series of words in the left-hand column, the object is to fill in the relevant squares with the shape, line, texture, colour or pattern that corresponds to and communicates the idea of the word. A final column for 'three-dimensional form' could be added

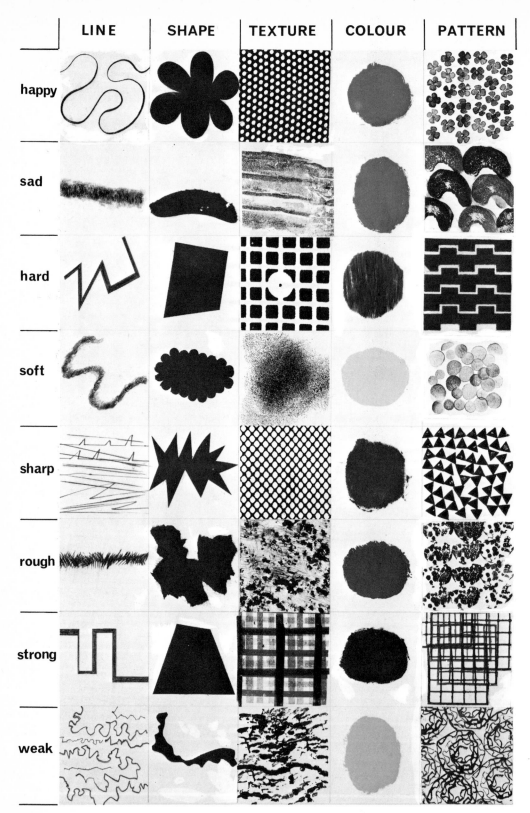

	LINE	SHAPE	TEXTURE	COLOUR	PATTERN
happy					
sad					
hard					
soft					
sharp					
rough					
strong					
weak					

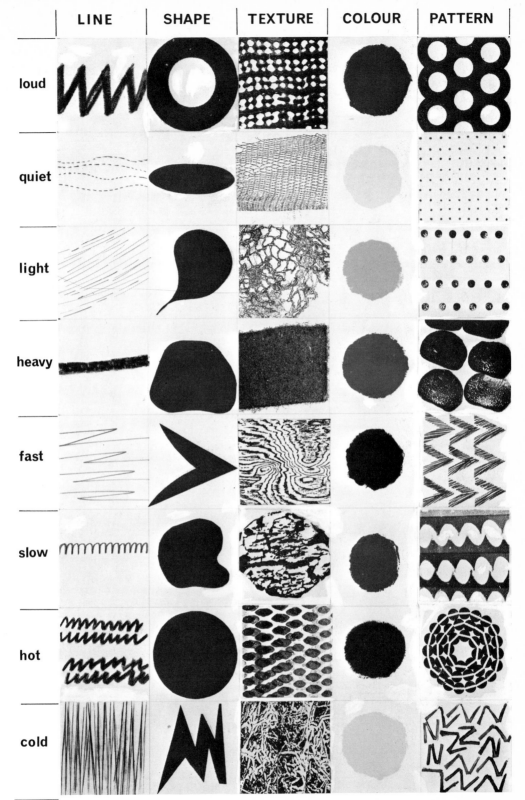

	LINE	SHAPE	TEXTURE	COLOUR	PATTERN
loud					
quiet					
light					
heavy					
fast					
slow					
hot					
cold					

94 to 98 *Visual communication charts and diagrams. These projects endeavour to give experience of drawing as a thinking medium in which actual information is conveyed. One important factor is that the evaluation is not in terms of the teacher liking it or thinking it is a 'good drawing', but rather in terms of whether the information being 'transmitted' can be read quickly and easily by the 'receiver'. These are critical evaluation terms. There is no point in the drawing unless it is more economic or efficient than the repeated spoken word*

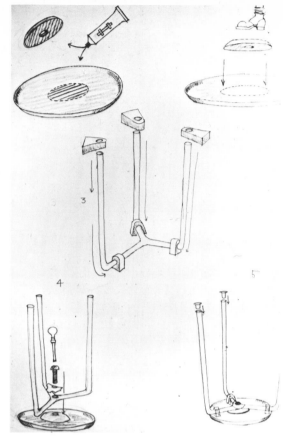

94 *A set of new stools are delivered to the workshop, they have to be assembled. This chart, part of classroom work, was drawn to show how the stools were put together and was used by everyone who helped in the work*

opposite
95 *A visual card index for use by younger children. The problem was part of a project to communicate a series of basic every-day operations in visual terms. Each process had to be communicated on not more than eight post cards, which would form part of an information resource centre for young children to use. The chosen process has to be analysed carefully and reduced to the fundamental stages. Irrelevant material is eliminated and prototype cards tested with young users.*

This project shows how design work could be used by older secondary pupils to help younger children and involve pupils in genuine problems of design and education. Such work is not limited to those talented few who can 'draw' in a 'picture making' sense. Communication is often more efficient when drawing is reduced to basic marks and becomes a communicative diagram

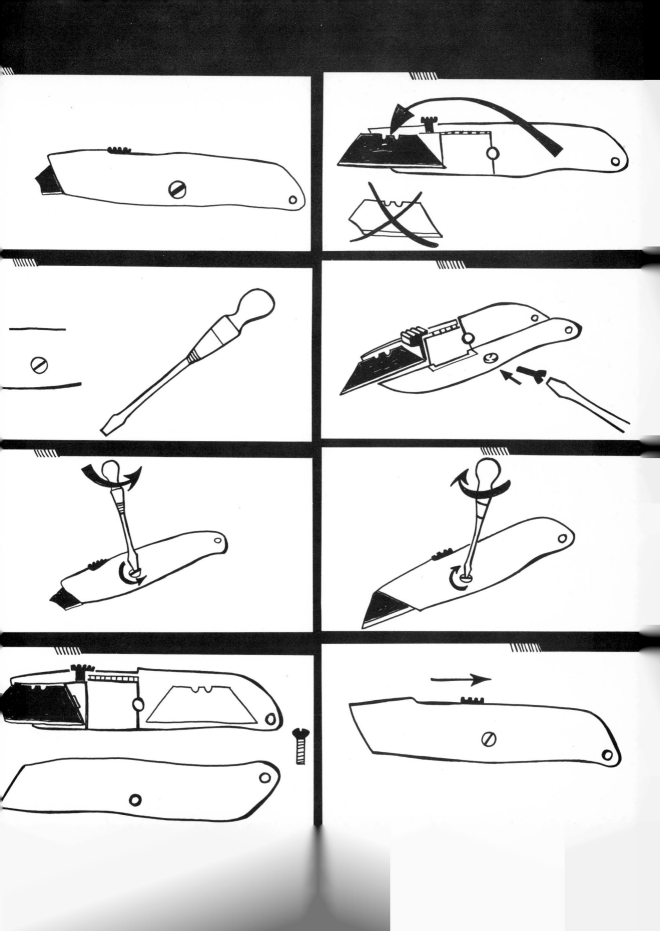

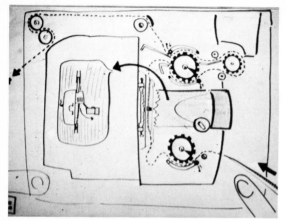

96 *Part of a series of communicative diagrams showing how to operate a film projector*

below
97 *A cooking recipe, by junior school pupil. Problem: to show, in minimum number of stages, processes involved in making an omelette. The evaluation of this visual game takes the form of another person cooking from these instructions*

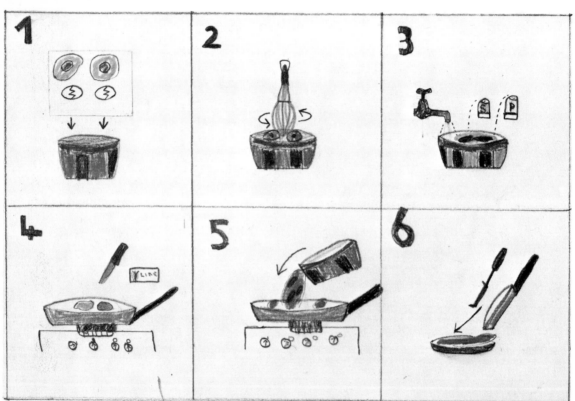

opposite
98 *Workshop design communication. Part of a project to communicate how to operate the band saw machine. One significant aspect of this problem is that the 'communicator' has to first study and understand the working of the machine before designing the chart. This work not only extends the pupil's experience but establishes a link between the art and technical departments*

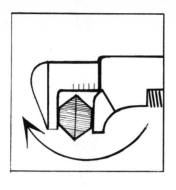 

 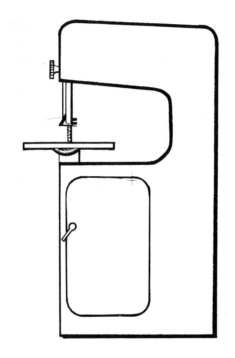 

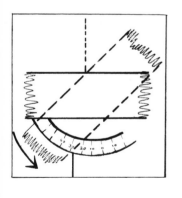 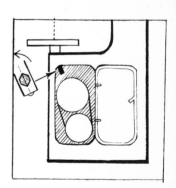

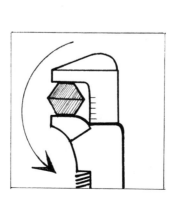

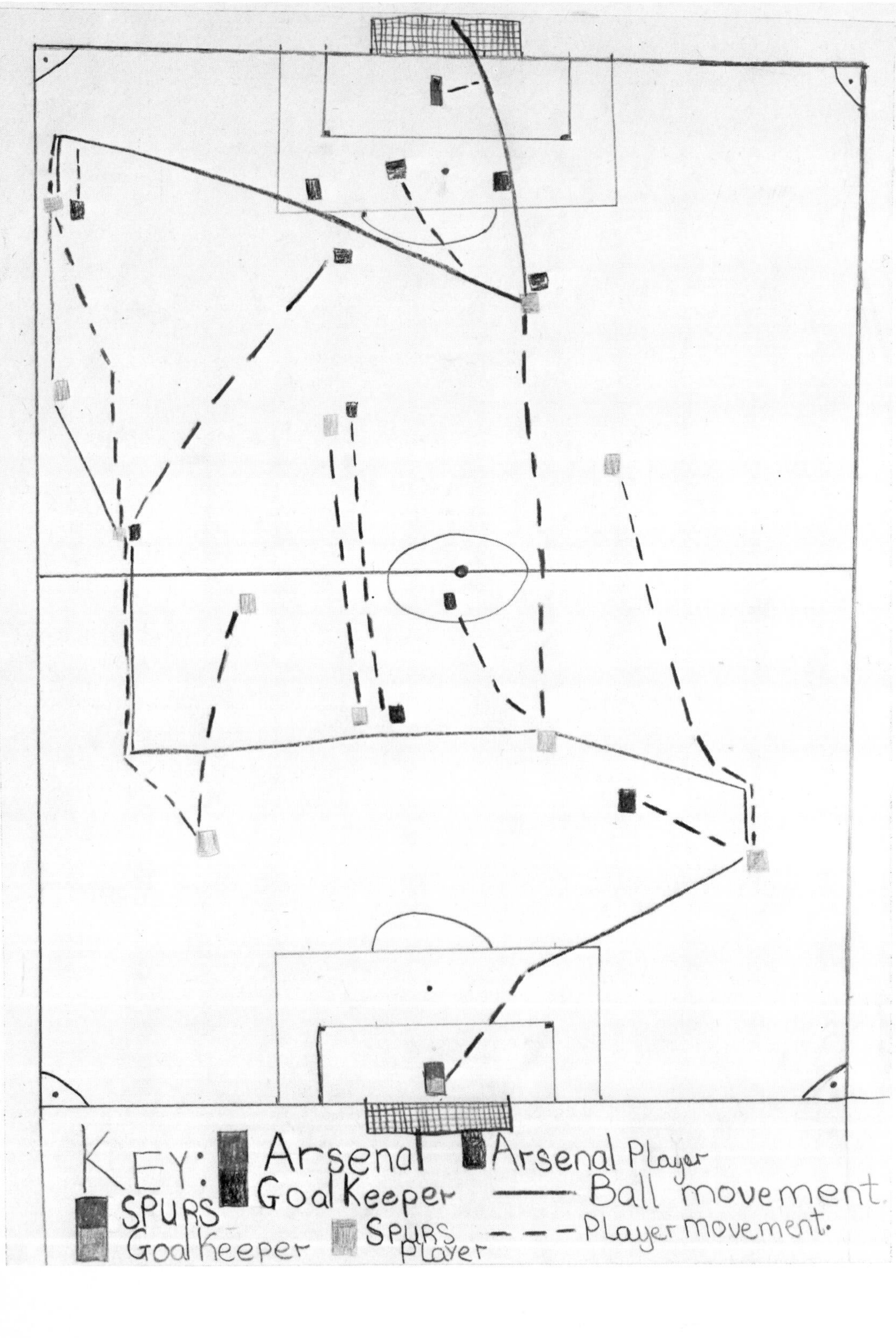
KEY:
Arsenal Goal Keeper
Arsenal Player
Ball movement.
SPURS Goal Keeper
SPURS Player
Player movement.

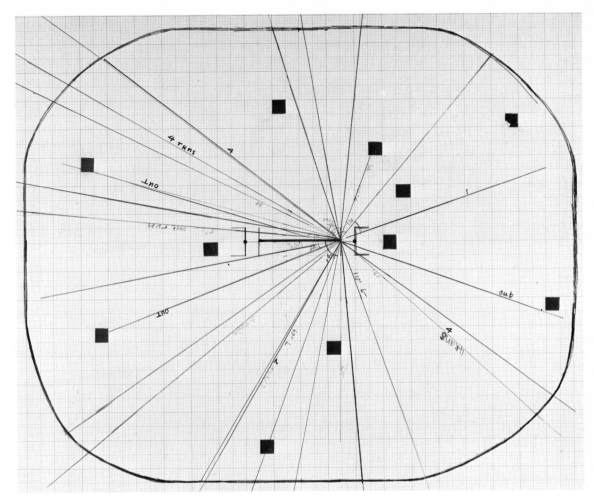

100 Technical drawing game. An introduction to the drawing and measuring of angles for young pupils, linking art with technical drawing (played in the art room). One side fields, the other bats. Numbers (representing angles) are drawn from a hat. The fielding side can move one 'fielder' before the angle is drawn. If the projected angle 'hits' a fielder he is out – if it misses, runs are scored according to the number of squares between the drawn line and the nearest fielder. If the angle is incorrectly drawn it is 'out', if the other team recognises the mistake

opposite
99 Reporting a football match visually. Part of a project with young children to discover the various functions of drawing as communication

TEE   TEA

PAIR   PEAR

ONE   WON

opposite
101 Ten-year-olds' work integrating studies in English with Art. A simple design game to illustrate the different meanings of homographic words

above
102, 103 A printing project designing symbols and illustrations for each school activity area

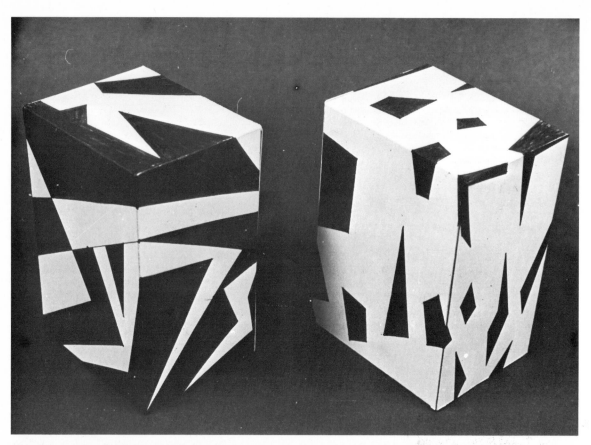

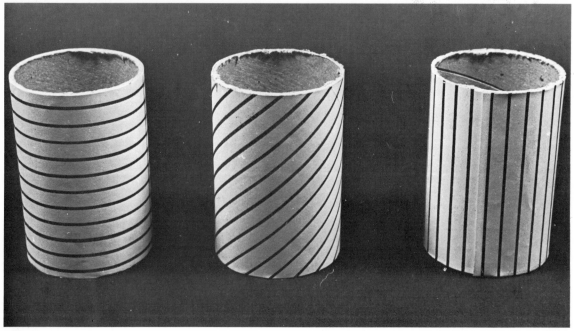

106 *Printing design project. The problem was to show in two-dimensions the different levels of an observed three-dimensional surface*

opposite
104, 105 *Study of the function of visual marks. Given objects of the same size the problem is to make one appear smaller and the other larger, using any visual device*

107   Paper stencil print to communicate the idea
of 'explosions'

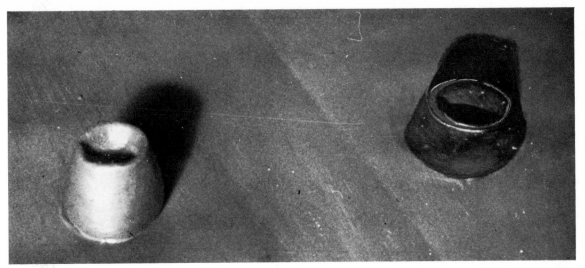

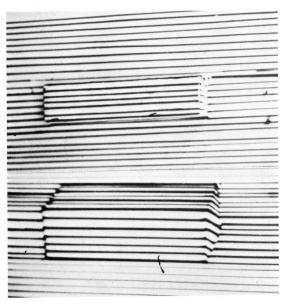

108, 109, 110 Various solutions to a problem concerned with 'visual mechanics'. 'Visually flatten a solid three-dimensional object and also try to project visually the same object from a flat surface'. A study in 'camouflage' and visual perception and into how objects are observed. In solving this problem it was necessary to establish a fixed viewing position

111   Visual symbols designed by students as part
of a test kit for visual perception and recognition

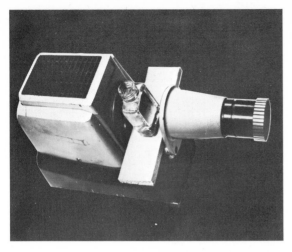

112 to 115   An introduction to projected imagery. No section on the study of visual communication would be complete without some reference to the study of film and ideas on animation. Using a standard slide projector, or any light source, images can very easily be created on a screen. Young children can be given sequential topics, such as the seasons or a simple life cycle and select the most appropriate material to make images communicating the relevant ideas, within a given time limit. 'What sort of shape, colour, line or texture will communicate this idea?' 'How long can this picture stay on the screen?' 'What kind of sound goes with this picture?' These are the crucial questions asked in constructing such a visual programme, and they are very similar to the questions asked in film making.

The process is immediate and very direct yet close to the idea of film where series of images have to be put together in sequence to communicate an idea

top left
112   Standard slide projector, showing use of the space between light and lens for placing objects or liquids for projection

top right
113   Making up 'slides' from scrap materials or fluids placed between glass or plastic sheets

centre
114   Projected enlargement of feather, showing how an object can be seen in a new way when projected

left
115   Projection of moving liquids. Light passing through small jar with paints and inks dropped into water.

The sense of visual spectacle is unique to the process, as is the capacity to see things as if for the first time when in the larger projected form

116, 117 *A useful area of study close to film making and animation is that based on the study of early optical toys. Such things as flip books, kaleidoscopes, zoetropes, and stroboscopes are very much part of visual study and communication*

right
116 *General view of zoetrope showing viewing aperture and other drawn bands in background. A zoetrope is a modification of the slotted disc device (see 117). A series of diagrams is placed inside a hollow cylinder (like a round biscuit tin). The drum is then rotated and the sequence of diagrams viewed through the slots in the side of the cylinder. The eye sees a succession of images giving the impression of movement*

opposite
117 *Phenakistoscope. A visual exercise based on an early pre-film making victorian toy. Flat disc has card 'handle' attached to centre. The disc is spun quickly in front of a mirror – the observer looks through the slits at the animated reflection of the disc in the mirror*

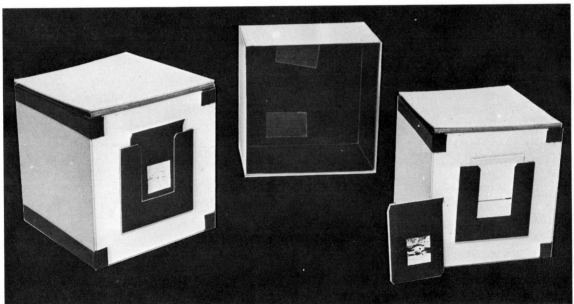

118 *Pin-hole camera. A simple experiment to introduce young children to the basic idea of photography. Such work logically forms part of a general programme of visual study and could include experiments with early optical devices such as the camera obscura.*

The two open ended cubes slot into each other to form a light-proof box. Photographic paper or film is held in position by the folded sticky tape on the 'back wall' of the box opposite the aperture.

The aperture is pierced through tin foil to give a more sharp and accurate hole. Alternative 'lens' using a horizontal slit also experimented with. The size of the box coincides economically with standard photographic paper sizes.

Lengthy exposures tend to be required but the results show, in a direct way, the underlying principles of photography

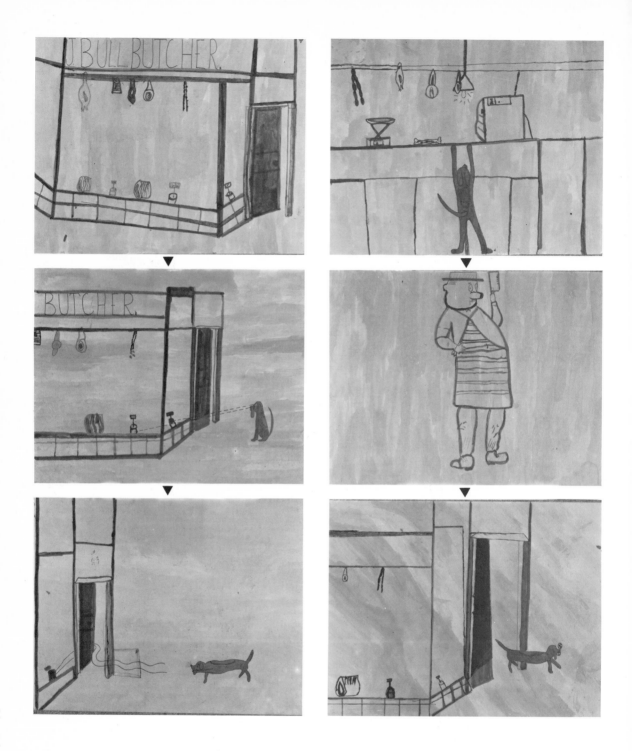

119 Basic film animation work with ten and eleven-year-old children. The aim of this work was to develop the ability to 'form a story in visual images'. Such an approach to 'visual' story telling is an important aspect of introducing film work to schools.

A series of paintings tell the story. The paintings are filmed using varying short bursts of movie film for each image. A Super 8 mm cine camera was used producing an animated film lasting some fifty seconds

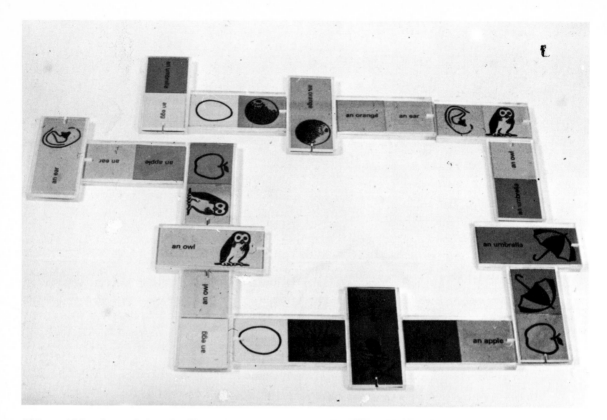

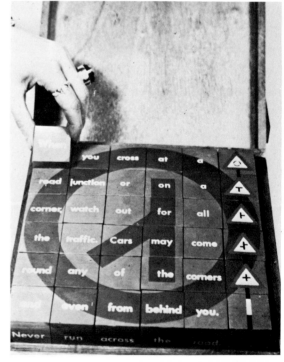

120 to 125   One of the significant functions of Design Education is the development of study projects to meet actual educational needs. The remaining illustrations in this section are of work of this type, usually long-term projects following initial study in problem solving, decision making and design methods. Such projects could well be further developed with older school children working with teachers and students to help younger children in schools. Teacher training students, working with teenage pupils and teachers make valid design teams for such work and open up potential working relations, while such activity in itself is a 'maximum yield' area for learning

above
120   Visual domino game designed to help young, language-deprived children. A visual communication project combining printing and constructional processes

121   Visual communications design study. Three-dimensional jig-saw designed to help young children, especially immigrants new to urban traffic, develop road safety sense

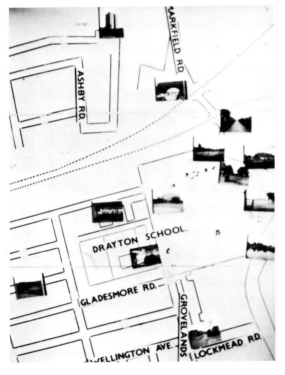

122, 123 Another secondary school project, combining work in the Art, Geography and Technical Studies departments, aimed at helping young, language-deprived immigrants

above
122 Enlarged photographs made into jig-saw puzzles as toys for young children getting familiar with the local urban surroundings

123 Photographic map of the locality

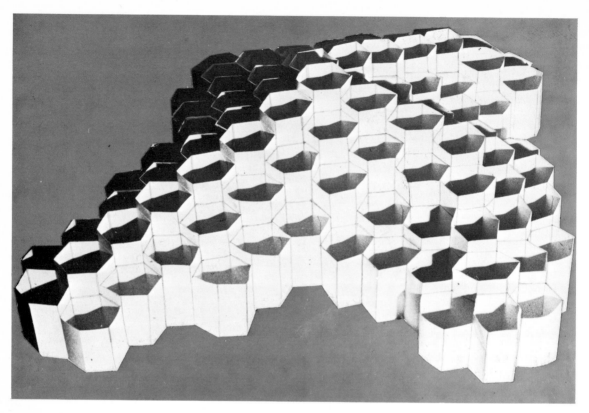

above

124   Art and science design project. Art room project to design relevant teaching aids and apparatus for science department. Design problem to communicate visually, selected cell structure systems. The form is 'beautiful' not because someone was trying to 'make art' but rather because it grew from an attempt to translate accurately the structural system, the visual quality is a by-product of the need to communicate information precisely

125   Art and geography design project. Art and design department involved in designing teaching aids and apparatus for geography department. Problem-solving exercise to design a device to communicate clearly to young children the 'idea of contours'

The scope for art and design departments designing teaching equipment for other school subjects (and their own) and younger age groups certainly exists. Such work offers ideal design problems and could well provide relevant programmes of work for older pupils. One significant by-product is that the senior pupil as a 'designer' could have a different relationship both with the teacher and younger pupils

Environment studies

It is important to stress that by environment is meant not just the hardware of our towns but all that we see, hear, smell and touch. Most of these environmental elements, that come to us through our senses, are man-made; whether it is the advertisements or films we see, the fumes we inhale, the noises we hear or the surfaces we touch.

Design education potentially embraces all these areas for it is concerned with the influence that man's decisions and products have on us and the form in which these decisions reach us.

Any genuine study of environment is therefore multi-disciplinary, while at the same time being centrally concerned with the design process.

Environment design studies touch all our lives and logically should form central integrated study areas including science, engineering, economics, politics, philosophy — in fact the sum total of our experience.

This section looks at possible ways of studying aspects of our physical world. It must be stressed however that this is a minute part of the major study area concerned with the impact decisions have on our lives, and our response and relationship to them.

The changing role of the individual in a mass, man-made society is the significant core of design education work. Design here is concerned with how and why decisions are made, how these affect our daily lives, and what contribution we as individuals can make. This underlines the idea that design education is too critically involved with major issues of life, happiness and survival, to be concerned only with artificial aesthetics or acquiring 'good taste'.

In looking at our surroundings more perceptively we need to become aware not only of the visual appearances of things but the forces at work behind them.

To look at our surroundings in this way it is obviously necessary to take 'design' work into a wider context outside the confines of the art-room.

Traditional critical 'good taste' values based on classic cultural traditions of static form and beauty are not necessarily the only relevant base from which we may now assess our surroundings. Twentieth-century technology has provided new complex forms and values. Value judgments related to rare concepts of beauty, form and proportion are possibly not the most appropriate bases for understanding the changing world or for the development of demanding critical responses.

Multi-disciplinary problem solving and the study of decision-making processes, are likely to develop more adequate forms of critical assessment.

We can no longer look at our environment and towns in terms of narrow needs, meeting the requirements of small groups. We need to look in new ways at the needs of people living in a changing scientific mass society while developing the capacity to assess the effectiveness of imposed decisions. Such study also requires the integration of scientific and rational attitudes with analysis, measurement, technical study and considerations of new human relationships.

Initially we may encourage a critical response, for more than anything else, we tend to accept our surroundings without question. We are not conscious of how they 'work' and how they affect life generally until they touch our daily lives at a basic level. We know when our shoes do not fit us but are less able to recognise when or why our surroundings do not fit our needs. Yet human needs can be identified and measured, and solutions proposed to meet these needs.

Until we can see our surroundings in these direct terms we will not be able to make sense of the complex forms around us. We sometimes disguise these issues in talk about appreciation of 'good' surroundings, tasteful choosing and 'beautiful' planning. At a simple level we could do so much by identifying our real needs and through experience of design problem-solving activity ask if these needs are being met.

We have a marvellous inbuilt ability to 'make do', though as technology's environmental influence becomes stronger our 'making do' becomes less effective. If traditionally we have only looked at external aspects of the world, beauty, style and classic proportions, we may have overlooked the critical need to assess the real effect our man-made conditions have on us.

As well as looking at appearances we do need to study all the reasons why things are as they are and in so doing develop a new critical code of evaluation, which would not be narrowly based on visual 'good taste'.

Developing a mass articulacy to our surroundings is a highly responsible job. Previous visual 'critics' of our environment have been a minority with 'educated' eyes, culturally orientated to recognise 'good' forms and with an understanding of traditional art values. We must endeavour to develop a wider understanding of the design processes underlying the production of the man-made forms around us. The interaction of the arts and science, is of course necessary for this and in many ways the existing divisions between such subjects has been the cause of much misunderstanding in studying the environment.

Design not only shapes the things around us but also shapes the way we live. Traditionally the so-called natural environment has been shaped by man's needs. Today, however, man can shape enormous areas of our world quickly and our industrial sciences can produce man-made worlds on a hitherto unforeseen scale.

The environment constantly evolves to meet changing needs. The rate of change is of course accelerating and our ability to understand our needs, and for design production to meet them efficiently, is crucial.

It is important to understand that our surroundings do not just happen by accident but are now very much the result of human decisions.

Efficient design solutions affecting all of us cannot therefore be left to accident or attitudes of taste. They must be based on very careful analysis of our needs, and considerations of the lasting consequences any solutions will have on us.

Naturally the needs of individuals in any society conflict and are not constant. Therefore design solutions are often compromises, or at their best, sufficiently flexible to be changed to meet widely varying needs.

Design studies related to environment attempt to identify the nature of some of these definable needs. Clearly at school level we may begin by isolating simple human needs within young people's experience, rather than considering all the many complex issues planners have to consider, which may be outside the scope of the school.

To have a value any problem-solving study must be concerned with tangible needs and capable of being tested. The learning really occurs when we can test for ourselves the solutions we have proposed. It may therefore be less worthwhile to engage in large scale, rather unrealistic exercises, such as designing a whole new town.

The problems and factors involved are so diverse and complicated that we could never genuinely evaluate our work, other than saying 'How nice it looks', a phrase that all too readily reflects the superficial level of much of our critical reactions.

All such pseudo critical assessment perpetuates a non-thinking attitude to our visual surroundings and does not encourage us to consider why things do not work, or alternatively why they positively contribute to the quality of our lives.

However there are many simple problem-solving activities related to genuine needs which are fundamentally about our surroundings and their effect on us. Identifying such problems, and the basic needs of people in relation to their surroundings, can provide the beginnings to the understanding of the wider effect and appearance of the world around us.

90

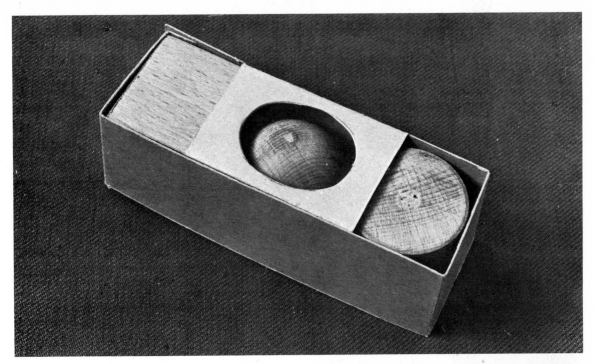

126–128 Problem-solving project concerned with the containing of objects. One of several learning factors was the introduction to environmental studies. Man-made surroundings are designed to 'contain' and just as we organise space to contain small objects, we also organise larger spaces to accommodate human beings.

The problem was to construct a container for three objects, (sphere, cylinder, cube) which would
(a) allow the objects to be recognised from outside the container;
(b) keep the objects in the container when it was dropped from a given height.

It was also necessary to obtain the maximum number of containers from a given sheet of card.

The last constraint was important as it was intended to introduce an economic element. Only one container has to be made up but it was necessary to show precisely how the remainder would be cut from a sheet of card, with measured minimum waste. This economic restraint clearly influenced the form of the solution

above
126 One economic solution to the problem

right
127 A further solution showing cut out shape. Although an efficient structural solution it was economically inefficient as only a few could be cut from one piece of card, with high wastage

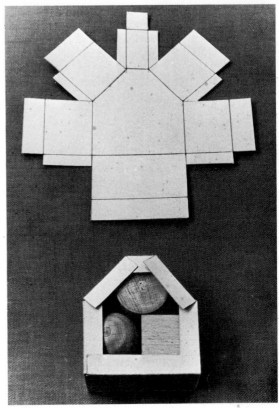

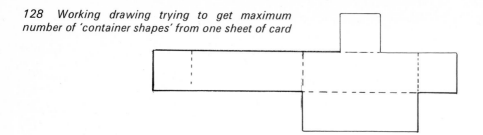

128 *Working drawing trying to get maximum number of 'container shapes' from one sheet of card*

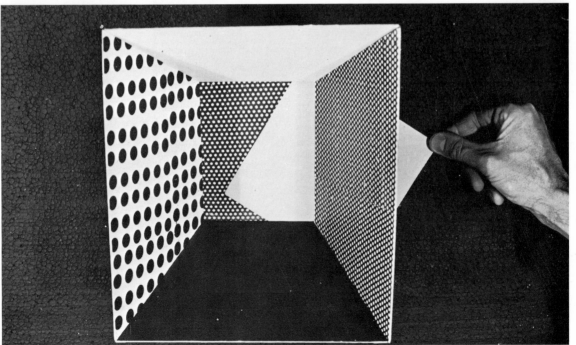

129, 130 *Design project to study how colour, texture and pattern influence our surroundings. The problem was to design a device to show how different interchangeable wall, ceiling and floor treatments would be appropriate to the needs of different rooms and locations. An additional learning aspect emerged in that the boxes provided useful ways of studying the effect and 'behaviour' of colour*

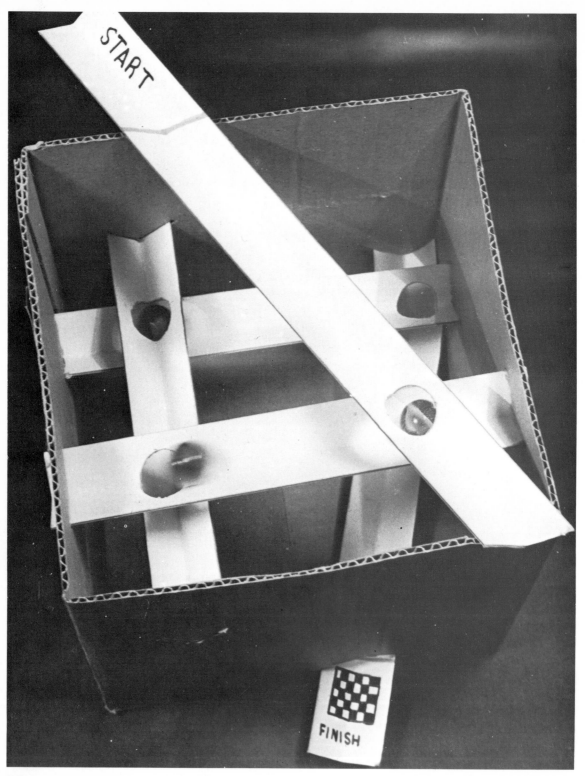

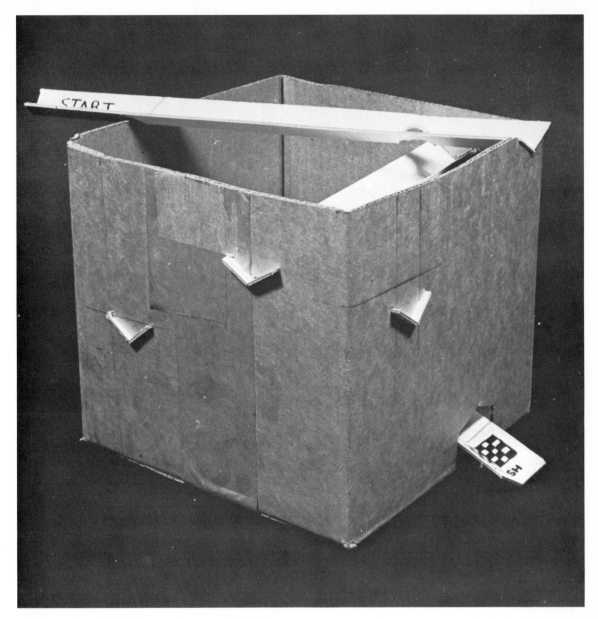

131 to 134 Basic environment study. The aim of this study project is to show that the 'behaviour' and movement of an inanimate object can be controlled and directed by a designed environment. This introduces the more important further study of how human behaviour is equally conditioned by surroundings

opposite
131 Problem to control the movement of a marble within a given time from two points. The flow control can be adjusted to the time requirements set

above
132 External view of 'marble environment' box showing structural slotting method

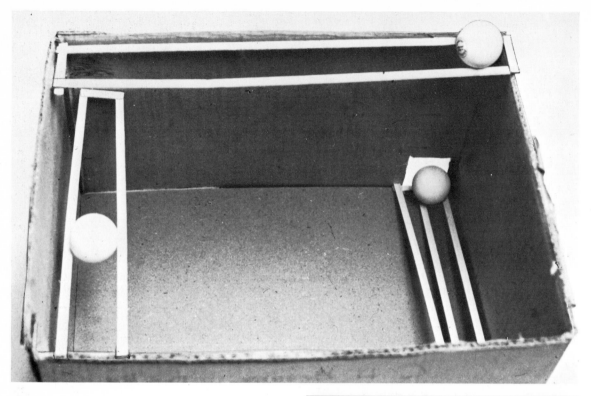

above
133 Solutions to problem of controlling the flow
of a table-tennis ball. Two points marked on a box
and the ball has to move from one point to another
in a given time

134 Two-dimensional solution to controlling
movement of marble

96

135 Having assumed that the 'behaviour' of inanimate objects can be 'controlled' by their environment, the next logical study stage is to examine how the lives of animate objects can also be conditioned by surroundings. An inter-changeable environment for a mouse. Part of a study programme investigating the environments of animals. The movements and habits of the mouse were analysed carefully, (using film, drawings and diagrams) and the surroundings were constantly adjusted to accommodate the habits of the animal

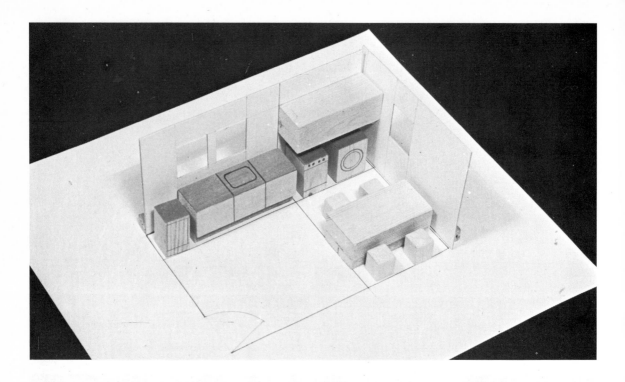

WINDOW

WASHING MACHINE

draining board

storage

SINK

draining board

storage

OVEN

FRIDGE

WINDOW

TABLE

DOOR

cupboard

opposite above
136 Interior design, environment study. Part of a project to re-design the layout of the kitchen in a school's domestic science flat. A model using moveable off-cuts of wood, cut to scale, to represent the space occupied by the kitchen components. This method quickly tested alternative organisations without 'artificial' and lengthy model making work

opposite below
137 Interior design, environment study. Study/ analysis charts showing door arcs and areas of operation required in the re-design of the kitchen layout in a school's domestic science flat.

The art department uses a typewriter as part of the general workshop equipment. For chart work the labels can by typed and layout organisation considered as part of the design process without any laborious lettering

138 Practical environmental problem solving. Organisation of space to accommodate human movement. The aim was to give experience of organisational design within constraints of a limited space. The problem was to organise, within a limited marked area on the workshop floor, the equipment needed for a kitchen for two people. Standard kitchen equipment was measured and cardboard boxes, drawing boards, scrap wood, cushions and bins were stacked up to these precise heights and sizes to represent ovens, refrigerators, sinks, cupboards, work surfaces, etc.

In this way no money was used on materials but an accurate assessment of space requirements, and human movement and measurement could be made.

Using such 'design methodology' it was also possible to adjust positions easily and to test all alternative suggestions and solutions. The working scale was realistic, rather than at model size, and genuine ergonomic and environmental problems were directly apparent

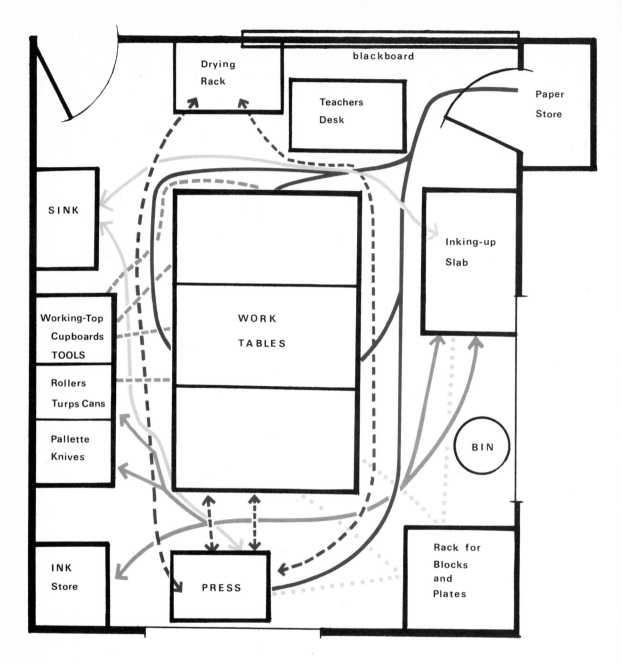

Drying Rack

blackboard

Teachers Desk

Paper Store

SINK

Inking-up Slab

Working-Top
Cupboards
TOOLS

WORK
TABLES

Rollers
Turps Cans

Pallette
Knives

BIN

INK
Store

PRESS

Rack for
Blocks
and
Plates

139, 140 Interior environment project. Design analysis programme for the re-organisation of print-making room in school art department. A long-term design project aiming to combine experience in analysing simple environmental problems and to develop an understanding of graphic design methods. Emphasis was placed, as part of the design problem, on the visual presentation of the information collected

139 Diagram, using colour overlays, to show major existing movement routes
The most used routes include those made with clean paper
finished prints
ink rollers etc
cutting tools etc
and with blocks to the rack and to and from the sink

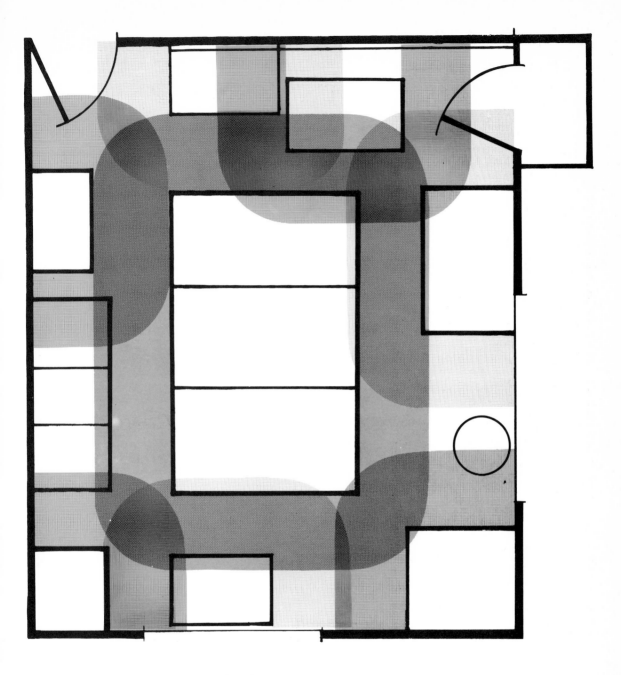

140 Colour acetate overlays showing the space needed to work around each bench, machine or sink etc. When all the overlays are placed together it is immediately evident where major congestion points exist

141 Design of a Prison Cell. Part of a design project to consider the needs of one particular type of environment. The initial stages of the programme included discussion of the special design requirements for a cell, with emphasis placed on security. This particular solution appeared not to be taking the idea seriously.

A coloured crayoned wall was added to represent a back projection screen with suitable changing images — to keep the 'prisoner' visually stimulated. On the walls a dart board and chess/draughts board to occupy him mentally, while on the floor a hopscotch court to keep him physically in trim. Such an approach appeared frivolous but shows clearly that the evaluation of any design solution depends on the particular priorities and requirements which have to be met. If the initial view point is that prison cells should 'punish', restrict and constrain, then it is clearly an inapplicable solution. If however the priorities were opposite to this and it was thought essential to take a humanitarian view of preserving 'mind and body', then this may be considered as an applicable solution.

This example shows how design should be considered in terms of appropriate or inappropriate solutions to problems, depending on various, and possibly conflicting needs, priorities and viewpoints

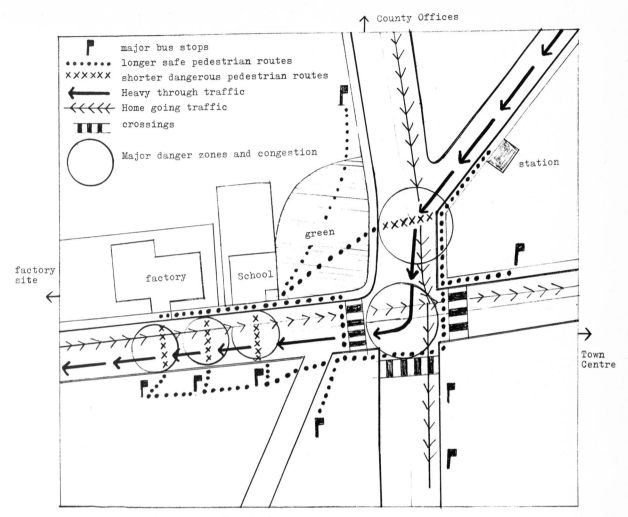

Legend:

- ⌐ major bus stops
- •••••• longer safe pedestrian routes
- ×××××× shorter dangerous pedestrian routes
- ← Heavy through traffic
- ⪡⪡⪡⪡ Home going traffic
- ⫿⫿⫿ crossings
- ◯ Major danger zones and congestion

County Offices

station

green

factory site

factory

School

Town Centre

142   Traffic/Pedestrian safety study project. Analytical charts of selected traffic complexes showing danger zones and patterns of pedestrian and traffic movement. In addition to the environmental design aspect of the project, it was also intended as a visual communication problem; part of the 'design brief' being to devise a visual method of reporting the findings of the survey

143 Town planning design game. A classroom activity designed to give experience of the major conflicting priorities and requirements town planners have to consider.

Each person is given a number of units (small cubes).

Different coloured units represent domestic accommodation, industrial sites, social amenities, schools, shops — all the things which require space in urban environments. The units then have to be placed on a given map and organised to meet particular conflicting requirements — such as maximum privacy for domestic units while minimising travel distance to work, or getting all the units into a very small space. The major learning point is that experience is gained of the basic problems urban planners have to face.

The game can be quite realistic if the scale between map and units is accurate and the relative number of units allocated for each 'amenity' (houses, factories, parks, cars etc) is based on actual locality study. For example, the ratio of shops, cars and schools to the number of individual houses

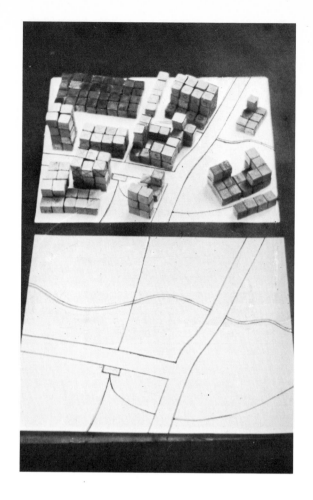

144 to 147 Environmental Design Study — Town Planning. Part of a combined subject study project of a small housing estate near school

opposite
144 Three-dimensional model of estate using off-cuts of wood. Simple moveable blocks cut to correct scale to represent buildings accurately could be re-organised. This was a focal point of discussions as locations could be 'moved' to solve problems which the survey pin-pointed

overleaf
145 Printed patterns forming map to show how areas of the estate were divided

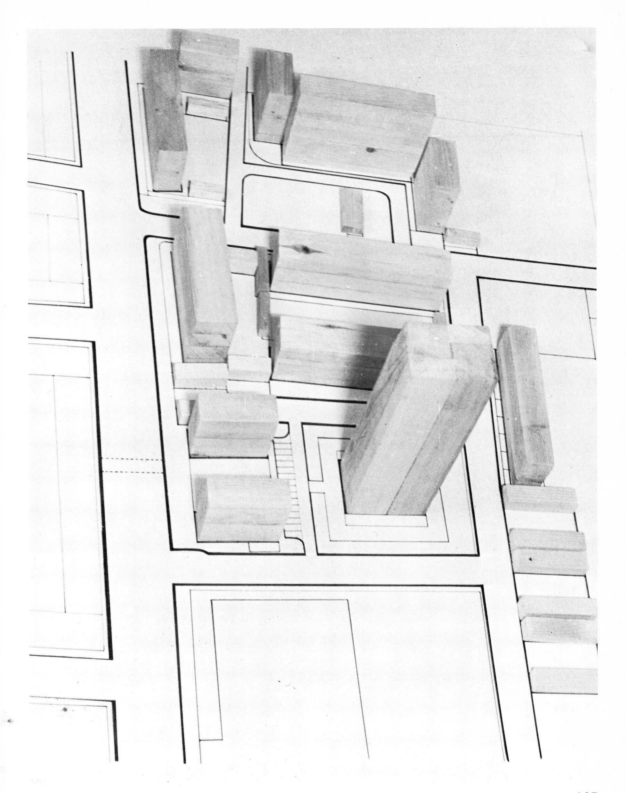

**Family Flats
with children**

**Flats for Elderly
NO children**

Shops

Garages

**Grass
NOT to play on**

**Muddy Grass
you can play on**

**Fenced Concrete
Areas**

Waste Land

**Rough Ground
with washing lines**

Roads

Parking

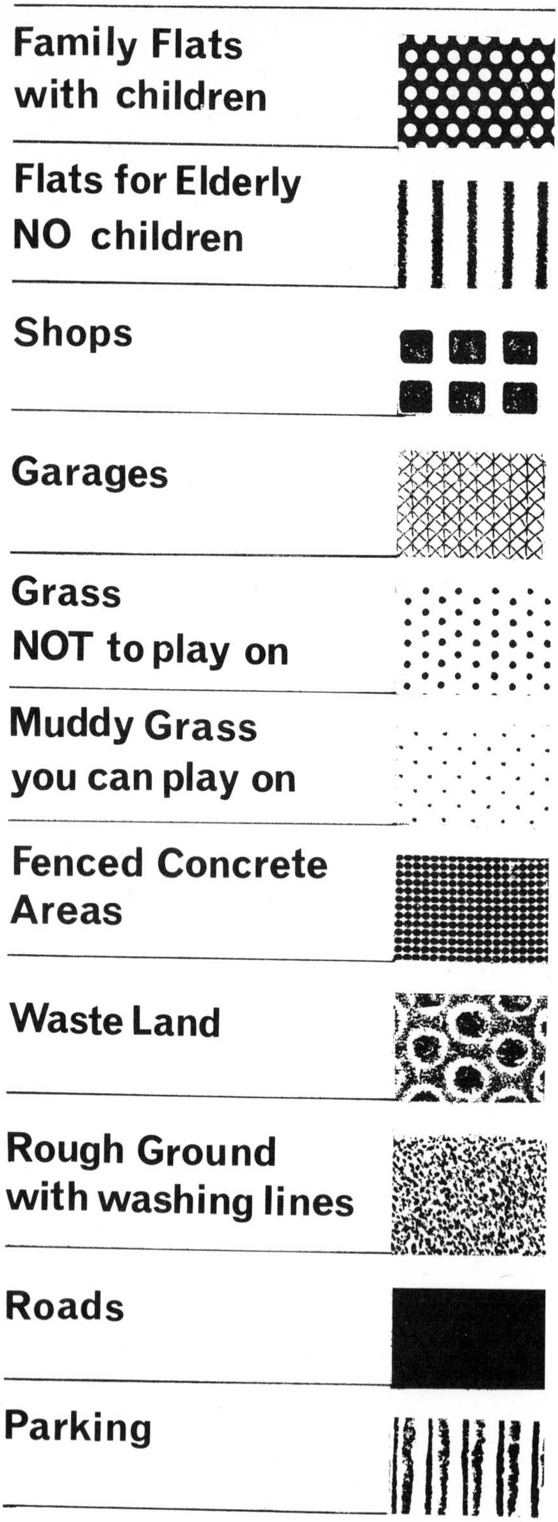

square metres

7000

6500

6000

5500

5000

4500

4000

3500

3000

2500

2000

1500

1000

500

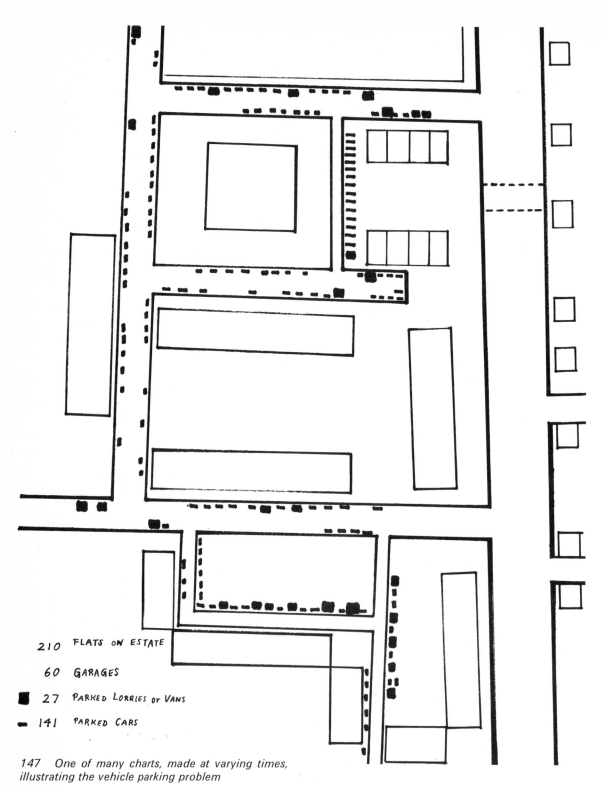

210 FLATS ON ESTATE

60 GARAGES

■ 27 PARKED LORRIES or VANS

━ 141 PARKED CARS

*147 One of many charts, made at varying times,
illustrating the vehicle parking problem*

Choosing and buying

Our industrial society produces vast quantities of goods. Mass production is one of the results of scientific and technical innovation and we live in a world of excessive material production – however unevenly this is distributed.

More and more manufacturers need to devise new ways of drawing their products to our attention. The competition for our money and our time becomes more hectic as more goods are produced. To help win this competition, and reach larger markets, the sciences of mass visual persuasion have been developed. The growth of new skills and techniques of visual communication are one of the by-products of our mass industrial society.

As the operational margins become narrower the visual techniques are forced to become more sophisticated. We are confronted with persuasive visual information in all forms of advertisements, packages and displays, and the pressures on the consumer are constantly increasing.

Design education is not narrowly concerned with 'consumer education' and it must never be confused with 'good buying' guides or casual consumer advice. However, the increasing impact of mass advertising and the pressures on choice making make it necessary to consider this particular area carefully.

Design education is clearly concerned with fundamental choice making at all levels and in all human situations. But the buying situation is especially significant, not so much for what one buys, but more because of the visual sciences used to dominate and direct our choosing and buying habits.

Visual education can in part help us understand the languages of communication and visual persuasion. We as individuals need as much help as possible to balance the mass of visual material 'attacking' us from the selling side of the 'choosing counter'.

Design education should not negate, in any way, the richness of spontaneous individual choice making, but should aim to give us some critical support when we are confronted by the ubiquitous nature of the mass society 'telling' us what to choose, where to go, and what to buy.

Choosing and buying is an increasing phenomenon of our industrial society. In re-examining the role of art education we need to identify all such major human activities and try to establish what can be done, to help us cope more readily with such situations in our daily lives.

We are very much exposed to the pressures of choice making in the buying situation. We are bombarded with visual material, and frequent illogical fashion changes disturb, or act against, any rational considerations.

Obviously the buying situation can never be a totally rational process and the reasons why we choose particular things will always remain complex and varied. But as the buying public becomes rapidly larger and younger we are faced with some responsibility to provide experience of how advertising and selling operates. Young people are possibly more susceptible to the fantasies and pressures of popular fashion and mass advertising than are older people. They are certainly major spenders in the range of popular consumer goods, and are therefore particular targets for visual 'assault'. Such young groups consume masses of visual material and permanent buying patterns are soon established. We are also forming buying habits which are not easily related to the habits of a previous generation. These habits may change even more but we must at least endeavour to give young people some experience of the basic processes involved.

Many aspects of buying and choosing are basically concerned with economics, and therefore with design education, as such factors are crucial to appearances. In fact a more realistic consideration of economic factors, as part of design work in schools, might help us understand more clearly the reasons for visual form.

Traditionally art departments and schools tend to concern themselves only with 'pure' ideas of visual style and aesthetics, ignoring the way in which simple economics critically influence appearances.

As an integrated study area the relationship of the appearance of objects to relevant economic factors would in fact be a logical piece of design co-operation in schools.

However this section is concerned with visual aspects of advertising and display and how it may help us make more considered choices in the face of mass advertising and changing fashion.

Advertising studies, market research work, or work concerned with economics, are usually located in school areas which have nothing to do with the art room. It is appropriate to consider how such work, within the framework of design education, could come within the wider scope of work in new art design centres. Much of the visual language used to attract our attention and buying potential is closely related to the problems of basic visual communication considered in the earlier section. Understanding how colour and images are used to get ideas over to us is very much part of this area of study. Familiarising ourselves with the techniques and intentions of visual persuaders, is part of the total understanding of the visual elements of our environment.

In nearly all design fields designers are identifying needs and requirements and providing solutions to meet these needs. In this area we have to consider widely differing types of needs. We have so far dealt with fairly tangible ones, related to functional factors communicative needs or simple everyday living needs. When considering the buying situation there are ranges of needs and preferences which are ephemeral and complex, and therefore more difficult to define.

We can, of course, with some commodities, clearly list our needs in strict order of priority. We can compare our priorities with those of the designer and arrive at logical choices. But in many choice areas it is difficult to define our needs. They may, for instance be very personal, as in the strong human need to communicate an image of oneself through one's design choices, and possessions.

In pre-mass-industrial times most people's needs were much more limited. Practical physical needs of survival were essential and little design effort was spent on 'luxury' commodities and recreation. However, our ideas of what constitutes a luxury change as our social economic conditions develop. With more free time and money we have discovered new 'needs'. Luxuries become 'needs'; we 'need'

to use our free time, we 'need' to relax or escape, we 'need' to decorate our surroundings and ourselves and 'need' to pursue all manner of interests.

These are needs in the same way as are more utilitarian commodities and it is essential to be aware of them. The advertiser and fashion designer certainly are and much of the mass media is of course devoted to attracting our money and interest into these new zones of human needs and areas of leisure activity.

Above all it is important in terms of design method, to recognise the many varying ranges of needs which are relevant to buying and choosing. These range from pure utilitarian functions to ephemeral 'fantasy' but the design process itself, meeting these needs, is common to all.

Understanding why we might choose something or why we might need it, or how we are persuaded to need it, are all part of a critical visual education.

We need to recognise the advertiser's skill as a visual communicator and the skill of package designers in point-of-sale advertising. We need to understand the organisational design skill involved in the physical and visual layout of supermarkets right through to the environmental artist's work in designing 'mysterious' boutique atmospheres to promote the social buying situation. All these are design activities operating very efficiently to promote buying and selling. The simple organisation and display of commodities, from fruit stall to department store, is a common everyday design activity, but one which has great influence on our patterns of choice.

Practical experience in simple fields of design problems, such as arranging objects to attract attention, are everyday activities (and obvious work for the art room) yet at the same time they are central to complex selling techniques.

It is obviously difficult within the limits of the classroom to simulate genuine buying and selling situations, for the necessary educational element of realism is absent without real money. But in the same way as simple environmental factors can be selected for study, basic problems connected with buying can be equally identified. We need to identify, as educational planners, areas of design activity for the classroom which are concerned with the same basic problems facing the buyer, seller and advertiser in the real world.

We can study what visual methods we can use to make things appear attractive. We can have experience of how to organise and arrange things so that they appeal to definable human interests, and study them in terms of shop layouts. We can study physical visual elements that produce persuasive buying atmospheres. We can analyse display techniques and the varying nature and influence of advertising. And possibly more than anything else, we can begin to study what our human needs really are — which ones are created by the advertiser and which ones already exist.

As with all other design study the programme of work is necessarily inter-disciplinary.

148   The profit game. A classroom activity designed to give experience of the visual and economic factors involved in the process of buying and selling. It is difficult to give genuine educational experience of this problem as the crucial ingredient, the use of real money, is usually absent in the classroom.

However this 'game' set out to simulate some of the basic considerations, and the various stages involved a wide range of topics. The object of the activity was to create the most 'desirable' object. This required 'market research' to establish what group members considered constituted desirability, or 'advertising' to persuade them that certain visual forms were pleasant and desirable.

The next stage was to 'price' all the materials to be used according to their 'desirability rating'. Each material was given a unit value. This was a lengthy process but involved valuable study into the communicative quality of materials. 'Desirable' materials were made very expensive and materials considered less attractive were cheaper. Each person was then given 100 'buying' units. The object was then to construct an object to communicate the idea of 'desirability', keeping a precise record of units spent on materials. On completion of the structure a 'sale' was held and the winner was the person making the maximum unit profit

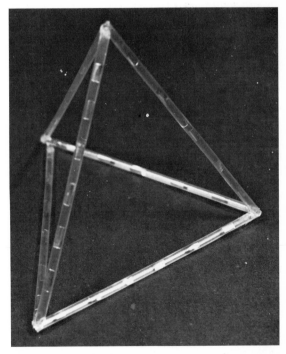

148   A 'winning' desirable object using one transparent straw with coloured segments of Mirroflex thread inside straw

The Profit Game Brief

A prototype activity to introduce pupils to elements involved in buying, selling and the processes of preference and choice.

Problem

Design the most *desirable* 3-dimensional object to fit into a cube not larger than 254 mm x 254 mm x 254 mm (cube *not* to be made).

Aim to produce the *most desirable* object to the *largest number* of the class or group (ie members).

Method

Each member of the group has to produce *one* object.

Each member has 100 units to purchase materials from the price list provided

Testing

The finished article is a prototype for sale by order to the rest of the group.

Each object must be priced. The selling price must equal the *exact* purchase price of materials, including wastage.

The profit is the number of units remaining from the original 100 multiplied by the number of individual objects 'sold'.

Accounts must be kept for audit.

Group members *may* work in pairs but would jointly be restricted to 100 units.

Newsprint free (*not* to be used as part of structure).

5 Units — 'Technical Consultancy Fee'

75 Units — Purchase tax on items assessed as 'jewellery'

1 Unit — per *one minute* use of machinery

10 Units — for use of *any* hand tools (including scissors and knives).

Official Price List

Unit Price	Item
10	One pipe cleaner
5	per 150 mm length clear *Sellotape*
10	per 300 mm of string
20	use of any one colour (paint)
15	Polystyrene, per piece (pre-cut)
20	per 254 mm square, coloured tissue paper
15	per 50 mm cube of wood
5	per 6 nails
25	per 150 mm square tin sheet
5	per drinking straw
1	per sheet of toilet paper
10	use of glue
10	per layer of *Plasticine*
2	per staple
10	per sheet of cartridge paper
30	per sheet of card
15	per 300 mm length of balsa wood
20	per sheet of card
10	per 150 mm square coloured gummed paper
10	per 1 mm square corrugated card
30	per 125 mm square of coloured acetate
5	per 25 mm of cardboard cylinder
10	per 6·45 cm *Mirroflex*
35	per 6·45 cm coloured *Perspex*
2	per gramme workshop waste (metal swarf)

149, 150 Package design with young children. One of the objects was to illustrate the idea of 'point of sale' advertising

top
149 Packages using lettering combined with simple impact images

above
150 Solutions to the problem of designing packages without lettering, to communicate the idea of the contents and make the relevant visual impact. Package on the left for fireworks, on the right for washing powder

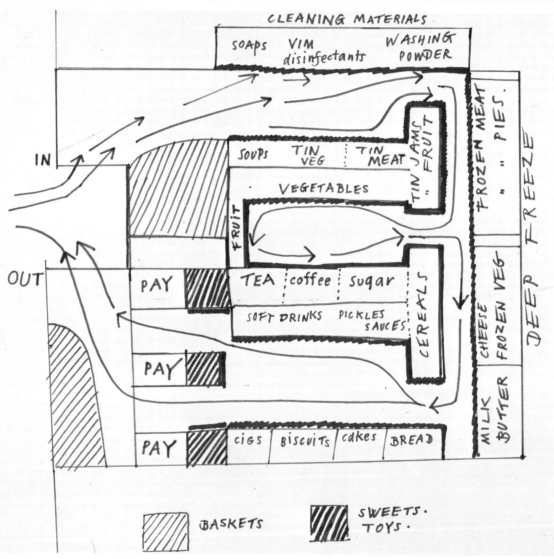

CLEANING MATERIALS

SOAPS — VIM disinfectants — WASHING POWDER

IN

SOUPS — TIN VEG — TIN MEAT — TIN JAMS " FRUIT

VEGETABLES

FRUIT

FROZEN MEAT " PIES.

DEEP FREEZE

OUT

PAY

TEA — coffee — sugar

CEREALS

CHEESE FROZEN VEG-

PAY

SOFT DRINKS — PICKLES SAUCES

PAY

cigs — biscuits — cakes — BREAD

MILK BUTTER

BASKETS

SWEETS. TOYS.

153 Stacking display problem. Problem set to design a cube that when stacked would form a repeating pattern

overleaf
154 Problem-solving project related to advertisement design. The object was, totally alter (reverse) the 'message' and essence of a given advertisement, using visual means only.

This required that the advertisement was first analysed and questions asked about what idea it was really trying to convey. Having established this it was next necessary to define how in fact the idea was conveyed visually. It was only after this type of analysis that an 'opposite' image could be considered.

In this example it was thought that the advertisement gave an idea of 'urban elegance' and 'evening sophisticated slimness'. It was then endeavoured to change this to a more comfortable rural feeling, with a thicker packet and less slim cigarette with a fresher outdoor image.

Advertising study of this type requires discussion on the use of words, ideas and language and how concepts are communicated to us in subtle ways. This project provided an opportunity for linked studies with the English department and social studies

opposite above
151 Colour pattern exercise. Part of a project examining the role of package design and impact of 'point of sale' advertising. The problem was to decorate each cube to give it major visual impact.

Cubes were stacked in different arrangements and tested by large numbers of pupils selecting the cube that first attracted their attention. The survey and testing of the visual impact of the cubes was completed in conjunction with the mathematics department

opposite below
152 Sketch diagram forming part of a design study into the layout and environmental organisation of self-service stores

SLIM KINGS
BRING ELEGANCE TO LONGER CIGARETTES
WILLS
pacemakers in tobacco
20 long elegant cigarettes
FROM WD & HO WILLS
26p
RECOMMENDED PRICE
SLIM KINGS

20 long elegant cigarettes
FROM WD & HO WILLS **26p**
RECOMMENDED PRICE

**BRING ELEGANCE TO
LONGER CIGARETTES**

WILLS
pacemakers in tobacco

**SLIM
KINGS**

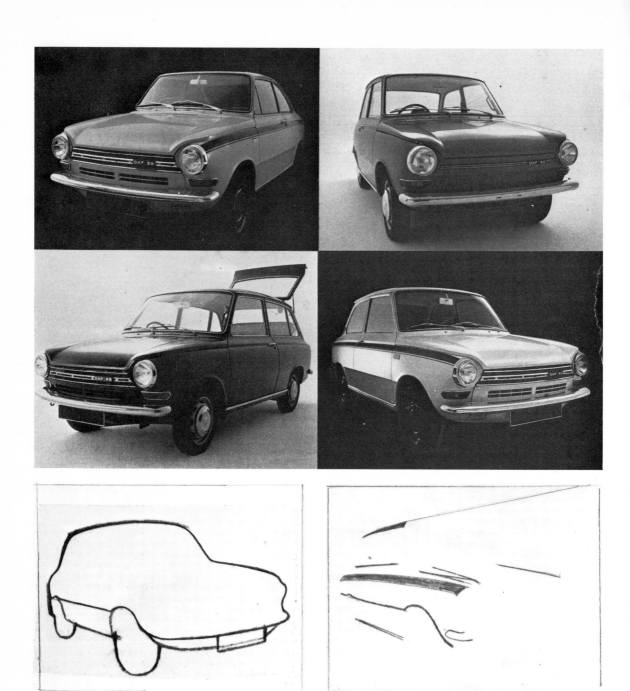

120

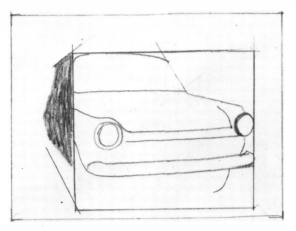

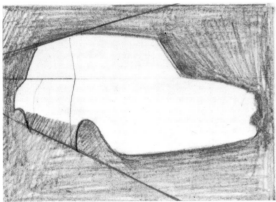

155 Advertising design study. Analysis of the various visual methods used to create an illusion of qualities that would help promote the image of the product. Part of the study considered how things can be made to look faster, smoother, larger, lighter, or whatever quality is required

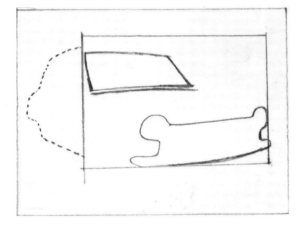

Daily Mirror	Daily Mail	GUARDIAN	TIMES

TOTAL SPACE	4700 Sq ins
ADVERTISING	1100
PERCENTAGE	23·5

TOTAL SPACE	5850 Sq ins
ADVERTISING	1900
PERCENTAGE	32

TOTAL SPACE	7500 Sq ins
ADVERTISING	1300
PERCENTAGE	17·5

TOTAL SPACE	8500 Sq ins
ADVERTISING	1400
PERCENTAGE	16

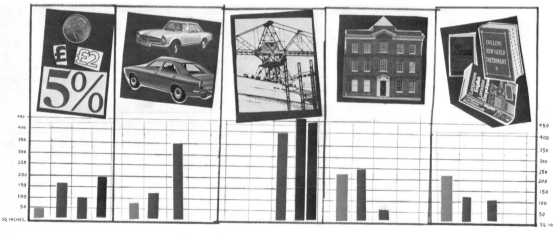

156 Newspaper advertising survey. A design problem to compare visually the advertising space for different topics and products in four daily newspapers

DESIGNERS & BUYERS
CONSIDERATIONS

CHAIRS & SEATS

● COMFORT

■ OPERATIONAL EFFICIENCY

▲ STRENGTH

Ⅴ CHEAPNESS COST

✖ LOOKS

◗ WEIGHT MOBILITY

157 Part of a design analysis chart. An attempt to classify visually the various design priorities and considerations for different types of seating

123

158 Visual style chart. A section of a light-hearted attempt to consider the communicative quality of objects and the relationship between visual style, fashion, human behaviour and choice making.

Potentially this design game clearly links art, English and social studies. It examines why we buy the things we do and the image we want to project of ourselves through our possessions

Summary of the future role of art education

The most significant consideration in making this brief summary, is to emphasise that design education forms only a part of any comprehensive coverage of art and design. Art is a wide and varied activity and design education is just one section of the subject's range of educational potential.

We may criticise the existing narrow nature of so much that is presented as 'art' but if all art lessons were limited to design education it would be equally restricting and unrepresentative of the full role that art should play in education.

Our ideas of what constitutes 'art', and what makes up the area of coverage for art education, are expanding. They expand in response to developing industrial and social patterns. Scientific/technical innovations spawn new human conditions and requirements, and new fields of technology explode the range of materials in which ideas can be communicated.

What constituted 'art' and 'beauty' was once easily and rigidly defined. But now, in a much more flexible society, the limits of what we accept as art are blurred and extended. Art is obviously not just about painting and sculpture; even what constitutes a 'painting' is challenged and debated and can include all manner of constructions, concepts, surfaces, visions and forms. The variety of activities and forms which now come within the category of 'painting and sculpture' alone is enormously wide. Previously we may have thought only of oil and watercolour for painting, and stone, wood, or clay for sculpture. Now in terms of materials the list is formidable, without even considering our changing attitudes to the manifold nature of sculpture or painting.

So art takes on new forms, and we think not only of new materials but new processes of image making. Film, photography, projected vision, electronics and the growth of technical structural skills all create new types of images. We also have the expansion of social climates and scholarship concerned with exploring new roles for art in society.

The role of artists, authors, illustrators and portrait painters changes in an affluent world of photography, film, advertising and television. Mass production alters our ideas about rarity as we see art forms from all over the world on our screens, and machine techniques alter our attitudes to craft skills. We need therefore to have a flexible approach to the 'arts' and to what new forms they may take.

One of the crucial barriers to creative education is the narrow static view of culture that we as teachers may hold. We may only recognise creative cultural activities when they are in the limited form of our own experience. Unfortunately the patterns of teachers' experiences are all too similar, frequently reflecting similar social class, educational and cultural backgrounds. This tends to put a straight-jacket on creative study and imposes restricting views.

We have a responsibility to provide young people with the widest possible view of the rich all-embracing nature of art, within which design education can play its part. Naturally in endeavouring to achieve this we have to consider changing roles and circumstances of operation. Here we come to the first area of possible change – that is the role of the individual teacher in a single discipline subject.

Art as a subject could for example include painting, drawing, individual sculpture and free expressive work at one end, with a wide range of traditional crafts, design study and rational aspects of visual education as a central core, and continue with photography, film and television work, to perhaps performing arts, design sciences, engineering and the structures of technology at the other end.

What is essential is that these activities should not exist in isolation, they must interact and form a total potential to creative work. No one subject is necessarily more important or endowed with more intrinsic creative merit than another. They are all part of creative visual exploration and study.

No one person, however wise and diverse, could cover such a range adequately without

125

dilution of the essential enthusiasm. On our own we therefore tend to retreat into specialisation, and children 'inherit' very small glimpses of what art can be. Such narrow views perpetuate misunderstanding, in each generation, about the real nature of art and design.

As a natural reflection of the expansion of our ideas about art and the development of design education, we may need to consider seriously working in teams where different specialist enthusiasms have an opportunity to interact. It is within new relationships between groups of teachers and of children, that flexible diverse work in art and design can develop.

The design process itself is a group activity and design education by its very nature requires interrelated attitudes.

In a changing world the need increases for constant personal re-assessment and the input of new teaching concepts. This is a real problem for the already heavily committed teacher. Isolated, over-worked teachers may find difficulty in gaining subject stimulus other than through rare external meetings or reflected ideas generated within the confines of the classroom. Groups of teachers working together, however, are more likely to generate an interaction of views. We have, of course, a long way to go in understanding fully the nature and scope of group teaching structures, but it is clearly one of the directions in which design education may naturally lead. If we are considering teams of teachers working together as a corollary of design work, we also have to consider the feasibility of more flexible groupings of classrooms and resources so that materials, workshops and equipment, can be readily available. Design study and problem solving requires finding the most suitable resources for the purpose. It may be that traditional, arbitrary divisions may not be appropriate if they cannot adapt to this essential requirement.

In design education the first priority is to study and identify relevant problems. From this stems the selection of the most efficient material, machine, resource or skill for solving the particular problem. This is a rather different order of priorities from, at its worst, studying a single craft skill, in isolation, for a given time before employing it to 'make-up' someone

else's 'design'. The skill of actually selecting the most appropriate resource, for the solving of a problem, is one of the new 'skills' inherent in design work, and in part replaces some of the emphasis on hand craft skills.

Such a change of emphasis may suggest open availability of all relevant resources, or simply re-siting some equipment to overcome artificial barriers and encourage the logical development of work. For example, some hand tools and light machinery might be located in art workshops so that studio and workshop concepts are combined.

The constituents of such groupings vary, but the more design is seen as a core activity concerned with human needs and decision making the more wide ranging the support subjects need to be. The removal of physical barriers between subjects is obviously necessary for discovery in design education.

As subject resources become grouped together and learning is centred on problem-solving enquiry, rather than imposed subjects, it may be increasingly unnecessary to divide our school days into the time compartments we know now.

A design project can logically involve many disciplines — mathematics, science, engineering, historical research, social studies, communications — and possibly each topic has more learning logic when identified within a central design problem than when isolated.

Any artificial development for the sake of a new label is at best questionable. To move over to 'open planning', 'inter-disciplinary enquiry' or 'team teaching', completely washing away individual classrooms and teachers, would be selfconscious and invalid. What is surely more advisable is a logical flexibility so that when it is educationally appropriate to work in teams it is possible to do so. Equally when it is appropriate to share resources, this should be readily and easily possible. However when it is better to specialise, or work individually, this should also be workable. There is always a dangerous tendency to throw everything out for something new. What is required is a constant growth of flexible attitudes and the resources to permit new approaches to operate.

So far we have looked briefly at the teacher's individual role, changing attitudes to resources, and workshop locations, together with ideas about lesson-time divisions in the school.

Other factors in this chain reaction are the role of the teacher as an evaluator and the nature of external examinations.

In a work situation with known set goals, where we distribute known solutions and require the retention of this information for future recall, the teacher operates on the level of external assessor. In a genuine problem-solving set-up the role changes. The evaluation is a collective activity related to the nature of the problem to which, there is no one known set answer. Rather, the question asked is — 'Is it an appropriate solution?' bearing in mind the already established requirements. Such evaluation processes suggest new forms of self-assessment and joint evaluation within the planned structure of design activities.

The emphasis of the teacher's role may change and genuine educational skills (rather than repetitive marking 'skills') could be used in devising and structuring problem-solving work.

Such skills are necessary to help identify needs at the outset and to ensure that appropriate methods of testing the proposed solution are built into the brief. As stressed in the Introduction, there are no 'bad' or 'good' design solutions as such, but rather inappropriate or appropriate solutions to any given problem. Efficiently organised problem solving has naturally built-in methods of evaluation, which can become part of the learning process, rather than a condemning or elevating examination mark. The more design education is centred around genuine problem solving the more necessary it will be to re-assess formal examinations and develop the educational use of self-evaluation.

We may therefore look for developments in art/design education which alter attitudes to the teacher's role, the equipment we have in art rooms, the structure of school buildings, timetables and examinations. However, any of these developments will be possible only when other external factors are moderated. Examinations are one external factor that affects the nature of work. A further influence is the public attitude of administrators, head teachers and parents to art as a subject.

It is probably true to assume that, while the cultural and social divisions exist which make art something separate, we cannot hope for far reaching improvements. We need to see the arts in all their forms — popular, performing and applied — working together in the context of a viable visual education. We need to consider the arts as central to our lives (and schools) and not 'hived off' with indifference to museums, galleries or once weekly lessons in the art room.

We tend to accommodate art and creativity in very narrow terms in both our schools and within society. We must above all recognise the many forms that art can take and ensure that they can be accommodated fully.

Prototype Plan of Design Education Work in Secondary Schools
With special reference to the relationship with other subjects and
consideration of design activity as a vehicle for learning

Initial Problem / Enquiry Area		1st and 2nd Years Some initial basic **Practical Problem Solving**	3rd and 4th Years Development of Activities	5th and 6th Years Development of Activities
Why do things look the way they do — Because of physical/structural function/material used/processes of making	Visual Studies	Construction Structural function problems of — Weight holding distance spanning joining space enclosing vertical structure mechanical movement material economy	Problems of — Construction with all available materials Joining/unit structure Machine processes Sculpture/modelling/Carving/casting Introduction to 3D Design Production	Industrial product design projects Engineering/Technology projects Design for 'Educational Equipment' 3D projects for identified 'consumer needs' History of Industrial Design
Why do things look the way they do — Because of the idea of information they communicate	Visual Studies	Communication Communicative function problems of — communicating ideas and information in two-dimensions and three-dimensions	Study of the Communicative Function of — Line/colour/shape/form/texture/pattern Problems in basic graphics Study of signs and symbols Diagram and chart making	Printing/Graphics Advertising Study History of graphic design and Advertising Basic optics and perception Photography Film making — animation History of the Development of the Cinema
How do our surroundings control/influence/effect/our behaviour and patterns of life	Environment Studies	Containing objects Organisation of space and area Control movement Control of inanimate objects Study of impact of colour/texture/pattern on environment maze environments	Study/Analysis of specific environments — Natural and Man-Made Interior environments Rooms/Workshops Basic Ergonomics Flow patterns/human movement Human operational needs Human Scale and the objects around us	Interior design projects Town Planning study Traffic/Urban development Social problems Pollution/population Environmental Design Architecture History of Architecture
What can we learn to help us understand the effect on our lives of — Mass media Advertising Buying/Selling Urban development	Social Studies		Visual aspects of Mass Media Visual devices of Advertising Practical study/survey and analysis of — Buying Shopping Fashion TV Programmes Films Magazines Advertising	Simulated design activity in — Buying/Advertising/Economic processes Study of processes of choice/persuasion/propaganda Mass Media studies/TV/Film Survey work on the influence and impact of mass media History of Fashion/consumer education

159 *An outline plan for an integrated design studies programme throughout the secondary school*

opposite and page 130
160 *A selection of introductory short-term practical problem-solving 'design briefs'*

Structural Function
Basic problem-solving activity

Practical problems concerned with why things look the way they do because of their physical nature, structural function or process of making.

1 (a) Given one piece of a selected material build the highest self-supporting structure.
(b) Using minimum material, construct highest structure which is wider at the top than the base, (at least three times wider).

2 (a) Using minimum amount of a given material, build a structure to span 45 cm while supporting the weight of one brick.
(b) Using minimum amount of given material, make a construction which will support the weight of any member of the group 45 cm off the ground.

3 Construct a form with ten identical units which can be extended in at least three different directions.

4 2D unit structure — construct a solid shape (No negative space between units) using a given number of units (15). Test by attempting to identify the shape of the original single unit.

5 Design an implement to fit inside a given container. The implement must reach every part of the interior form. Test by extracting given contents without waste.

6 Support a given weight off the ground at the farthest point (measured along the ground) from a fixed point (base).

7 Produce the maximum number of identical containers from a single given sheet (paper, card). The container to hold three given objects. The shape of all objects to be identified externally.
    Test structure of container by dropping from given height.
    Construct one, but show precisely how remainder are extracted from initial sheet.

8 Human ergonomics — 3D. Design a sleeved garment for the upper half of the human body using minimum amount of given material which will fit all group members.
    The 'garment' must allow a given physical movement (tie shoe laces) to be performed without damaging the structure.

9 (a) Construct a device to transfer movement from one plane to another plane.
(b) Construct a device to transfer circular motion to reciprocal motion.

10 Totally enclose a given irregular 2D plan to a minimum central height of 10 cm using the minimum amount of material.

Communicative Function
Basic problem-solving activity

Practical problems concerned with why things look the way they do because of the idea or information they communicate.

1 '3D Chocolate Box'
Model to communicate, in non-literal forms, the following flavours — nut, salt, lemon, peppermint, mustard, pepper.

2 Model a 'container' which communicates the nature of the contents. Either work from the advertisement copy for a selected container, or from given classification of contents.

3 Visually flatten a 3D object. Project visually the illusion of the same object from a flat plane.

4 Given three identical containers make one appear larger and one smaller than the original.

5 Communicate in vision only given process or instructions:

    (i)   Assembly and function of car engine part
    (ii)   Technical workshop/machine process
    (iii) Loading camera or tape recorder
    (iv)   Mending fuse or changing electric plug
    (v)   Cooking recipe.
    Course members admit 'areas of ignorance' and test visual instructions on relevant course members.

6 Visual communication charts
(a) Complete word/vision grid chart
Vertical column of descriptive words
Horizontal headings — colour, line, texture, form, shape.
(b) Colour — Line/Shape communicative problem
The most appropriate angle for a particular colour
The most appropriate shape for a particular colour.

7 Vision—sound game
'Write' played linear sounds. Read back and test.

8 Translate a linear cross-section into a flat surface. Use only one visual element (line, texture, colour, etc). Test by returning to cross section.

9 Totally reverse the 'message' of a given advertisement, using visual means only (eg colour, texture etc).

10 Select from a magazine advertisement an object, cars, containers, etc. Explore any visual devices which can alter their factual nature — ie make them appear larger, softer, smoother, younger, more attractive, etc.

11 Visual reporting of football game
Either translate a written report or design a visual system for specific observed event.

Environmental Study
Basic problem-solving activity

Some practical design study of towns and interior living spaces. All the problems are short term whereas the topic possibly requires more long term projects.

1 Analysis of existing environment
Using visual form (chart or model) study how a practical workshop or room is used
Study layout and make suggestions for improvement
How does existing organisation effect:
 (i) working efficiency
 (ii) safety
 (iii) movement
 (iv) noise

2 Devise a visual method of analysing existing traffic complex
Special reference (i) Efficiency of traffic flow
(ii) Pedestrian safety

3 Hypothetical town planning problem
Organise within a rectangle 20 cm × 25 cm the following units. Each unit is a 1 cm cube
100 living units (25 for old people, 25 for single, remainder family units)
 15 shopping units
  4 school units, 1 hospital unit
  6 amenity units (cinema, church, library, etc)
 20 open space units, (parks, etc)
 50 work units (35 heavy units, 15 light industry)

Consider minimum travel distance (to services and work) and privacy as the top priorities (25% work outside area travelling by train. 75% work locally)

4 Internal environments
(a) In a given cardboard box build an environment to control the movement (directional behaviour) of a marble or table-tennis ball. Work within constraint of a given time for ball to move from entry to exit point
(b) Organisation of limited space (life size)
 Mark out, on the floor, an area 2 m × 3 m to accommodate either:
(i) the components and functions of a family kitchen
(ii) the following activities for two people — eating, sleeping, working, cooking, etc
 Use cushions, cardboard boxes, drawing boards etc to define the precise areas within which to operate

(c) Colour and surface
 Paint the interior of a cube with the most appropriate colour and surface pattern for:
 (i) Dentists waiting room
 (ii) Long term detention cell
 (iii) Hospital ward
 (iv) Children's playroom.

opposite and overleaf
161–163 Plans illustrating how authorities are approaching the integration of art and design departments. It is significant that new solutions to the building of schools reflect new ideas and attitudes to timetables, classroom structure and learning and teaching techniques. The layouts reflect the need for logical relationships with relevant subjects and a concern with flexible organisation, necessary for design and problem-solving work

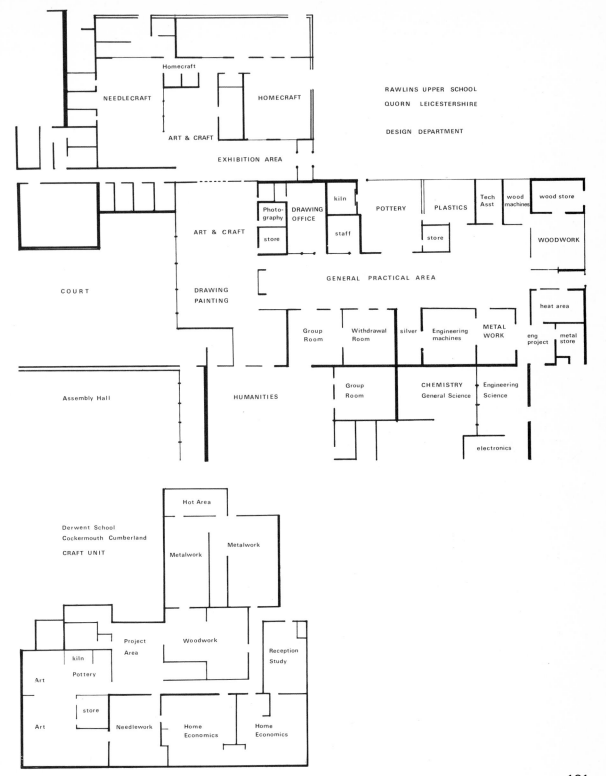

RAWLINS UPPER SCHOOL

QUORN LEICESTERSHIRE

DESIGN DEPARTMENT

Homecraft

NEEDLECRAFT

HOMECRAFT

ART & CRAFT

EXHIBITION AREA

Photo-graphy

DRAWING OFFICE

kiln

POTTERY

PLASTICS

Tech Asst

wood machines

wood store

store

staff

store

WOODWORK

ART & CRAFT

GENERAL PRACTICAL AREA

COURT

DRAWING PAINTING

heat area

Group Room

Withdrawal Room

silver

Engineering machines

METAL WORK

eng project

metal store

Assembly Hall

HUMANITIES

Group Room

CHEMISTRY

General Science

Engineering Science

electronics

Derwent School
Cockermouth Cumberland

CRAFT UNIT

Hot Area

Metalwork

Metalwork

Project Area

Woodwork

Reception Study

kiln

Pottery

Art

store

Art

Needlework

Home Economics

Home Economics

JACK HUNT SCHOOL
PETERBOROUGH

Upper School

Homecraft

staff group

Needlework area

kitchens

DESIGN
Resources

Woodwork

wood store

Textiles

PAINTING

Drawing

Craft

Reference

Resources
Study

Projects

metal store

Heat
Treatment

dark room

kilns

Pottery

glazing

Metalwork

Engineering

to SCIENCE and
MATHEMATICS
departments

General Certificate of Education   Advanced Level
A83 Design

The examination consists of two theory papers, each of three hours' duration, and an assessment of the candidates' course work by a visiting examiner. The course work carries 60% of the total marks for the examination.

Candidates are expected to acquire a general understanding of the functions of a designer at the level appropriate to sixth form studies. (A designer is taken to mean anyone who consciously seeks to determine some part of a man's environment in a way most suitable to man's purpose.) The syllabus therefore, is concerned with the physical, rational and emotional nature of man, as well as with the shaping of materials and the production of well-designed goods within the total environment.

Paper I
Man as an individual
Human dimensions; averages and ranges

Some awareness of the importance to the designer of human capacity by reference to: (a) general knowledge of the skeleton with particular reference to joints and muscles and their degree of movement; (b) simple outlines of the circulatory, respiratory and nervous systems; (c) bodily needs regarding nourishment and atmosphere; (d) bodily tolerances regarding temperature, light and sound; (e) fatigue associated with (a), (c) and (d).

The senses: voluntary and involuntary activities.
Some understanding of human emotions and needs.

continued on next page

Man in Society
Environment, natural and man-made; the social organisations, past and present, which help to reconcile man and the physical world he inhabits. Transport and traffic. The various means for the communication of ideas. The social significance of the designer in seeking to produce a physically, emotionally and aesthetically satisfying environment with the aid of technological advances.

Production and economics. The relationship between methods of production, social organisation and the character of the resulting artefacts (from handwork to the industrial revolution and automation). The relationship between the community (the user), industry (the maker) and the designer. Market research. Advertising and obsolescence. The impact of science and technology on social organisation.

The consumer in an industrial society. Mass production and quality. Consumers' problems and the development of consumer protection groups. Opportunities and limitations inherent in artefacts produced for a mass industrial society.

Paper II
The designer and his resources
A general understanding and some experience of available materials and processes and their use in architecture and industry. (This range of materials should include wood, metals, ceramics, glass, concrete, paper, cardboard, plastics, rubbers and textiles.) Comparative qualities of materials, eg, hardness, strength in tension or compression.

Candidates should undertake a more detailed study of at least one of the following categories of materials.

(i) Wood. (ii) Ferrous and non-ferrous metals and their alloys. (iii) Ceramics.

Course work
Candidates must submit a specific design project as the major part of their course work, but in addition they must also have available course work showing general investigations of visual, tactile, spatial and structural qualities, including evidence of design procedures, enquiries and critical appraisals undertaken.

Each candidate must present his project as a sufficiently finished piece of work (or as a design prototype), supported by documentation, including a statement of the problem, preliminary sketches, calculations and adequate working drawings to indicate the extent to which he has understood the problem, his approach in trying to solve it, and his ability to follow the work through to a conclusion. The candidate must be prepared to discuss all aspects of this work with the visiting examiner and to answer questions orally about it.

164   An extract taken from the syllabus of the first General Certificate of Education, Advanced Level Design Paper (Oxford Delegacy of Local Examinations 1971). The production of this syllabus was a significant stage in the development of design education. It is intended that the scope of this paper will be extended to accommodate other areas of design

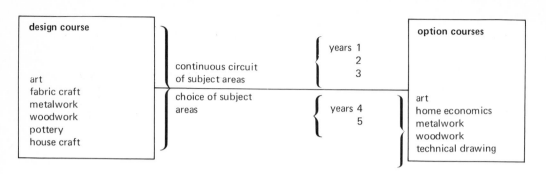

Years 1 and 2 are introductory and exploratory for both the five year Design Course and the various option courses.

Basic study areas include :
1 Development of personal language of visual communication (two and three-dimensions)
2 Study of relationship between ideas and materials.
3 Aspects of perception including colour/light theory.
4 Introduction to ergonomics and design methodology.

Year 3 is a continuation of the introductory course leading to more specialised options in year 4.

Year 4 and 5 are concerned with studying basic aspects of the man-made environment. The aim is to provide individuals with the opportunity to discover the means best suited to their interests and abilities for investigating, analysing, evaluating and commenting on aspects of the social and physical world manifest in visual/functional terms.

The main areas of study include :
1 Communications
Advertising – relationship between fine art and advertising – display – exhibition design – packaging
Relationship between visual and verbal communication.
Mass media – television film and photography.

2 Living and working space
Requirements in terms of space, light, colour, heating, ventilation
Survey of alternative requirements in other parts of the world
The modifying influence of geography on the design of buildings. Relationship of living and working space – family unit and urban organisation. The needs of transport.

3 Human aids and extensions
Clothing – fashion – tools – furniture
Specialised forms of transport – play equipment

This list is intended as a guide and can be modified or added to under the general headings.

continued on next page

Each candidate must provide :

1   evidence that he/she has attempted one project from each area of enquiry
2   evidence of work on a final project, selected from one or more of the areas
3   a coursework diary/sketchbook.

Assessment procedure

We are anxious to assess work in a way that is in sympathy with the character of these proposals and it therefore seems appropriate to use criteria directly connected with the work submitted. Basically, the work consists of a combination of intellectual and practical skills. The universal design approach which utilizes these skills offers the basis for both structuring the work and organising the assessment.

Candidates will therefore base their coursework and final projects on the following five stages, each of which will have an assessment value.

1   State the problem (coursework diary)
2   Collect and process information
3   Develop and communicate idea (including interview with project tutor and display for assessment)
4   Produce a solution
5   Evaluate design produced, test against brief.

165 Part of a proposed Design Syllabus for the Certificate of Secondary Education (Mode 3), drafted by Michael Swain, Head of the Department of Creative Activities, Sheredes School, Hoddesdon, Hertfordshire.
This syllabus forms part of a 'common core' course for all pupils in a school where the curriculum is organised in seven broad areas, followed by everyone for the first five years. It is intended that this syllabus could form the basis for both the Certificate of Secondary Education (Mode 3) Design Paper and a General Certificate of Education 'O' level Design Examination

Bibliography

Magazines journals and pamphlets

Bulletin for Environmental Education
Education Unit, Town and Country
Planning Association, London

Newsletter The National Association
for Design Education

Studies in Design and Craft Education
published twice yearly

Look Out BBC TV series, Design and the
Environment, Teachers notes by John
Prescott Thomas and Peter Green BBC
Publications 35 Marylebone High Street W1

Design Magazine Design Council

Architectural Design London

Screen and Screen Education Society
for Education in Film and Television

Built Environment Architecture and
Planning Publications Ltd, London

Journal Royal Institute of British
Architects, London

The Ecologist London Ecosystems Ltd

Newsletter The National Association for
Film in Education

Practical Education and School Crafts
The Journal of the Institute of Craft
Education

The Designer Journal of the Society of
Industrial Artists and Designers

Books

Bagrit, L, **The Age of Automation**
Weidenfeld and Nicholson 1965

Banham, R, **Guide to Modern
Architecture** Architectural Press 1962

Banham, R, **Theory and Design in the
First Machine Age** Architectural Press
1970

Baynes, K, edited by **Attitudes to Design
Education** Lund Humphries 1969

Cook, P, **Architecture: action and plan**
Studio Vista 1967

Crosby, T, **Architecture: City Sense**
Studio Vista 1965

Cullen, G, **Townscape** Architectural
Press 1961

Dreyfuss, H, **Measure of Man** New
York Grossman (revised edition)

Field, D, **Changes in Art Education**
Routledge Kegan Paul 1970

Fletcher, A, and others **Graphic Design:
visual comparisons** Studio Vista 1965

Gregory, R, **The Intelligent Eye**
Weidenfeld and Nicholson 1970

Healy, S, **Town Life** Batsford 1968

Heath, R B, **The Mass Media** (4 volumes)
Nelson 1968–1969

Hennessey, R, **Transport** Batsford 1966

Hoskins, W G, **The Making of the
English Landscape** Penguin Books (new
edition) 1970

Jones, C, **Design Methods** J Wiley 1970

Kepes, G, edited by **Vision and Value
Series** Studio Vista 1966 Education of
Vision The Nature and Art of Motion
Structure in Art and in Science Module,
Symmetry, Proportion The Man-made
Object Sign, Image, Symbol

Laughton, R, **TV Graphics** Studio Vista
1966

McLuhan, M, **The Mechanical Bride:
folklore of Industrial man** Routledge
Kegan Paul 1967

Maxwell Fry, E, **Art in a Machine Age** Methuen 1970

Mayall, W H, **Machines and Perception in Industrial Design** Studio Vista 1968

Meller, J, edited by **The Buckminster Fuller Reader** Penguin 1970

Melly, G, **Revolt into Style: Popular Arts in Britain** Penguin Books 1972

Mumford, L, **The City in History** Penguin Books (new edition) 1966

Nairn, I, **Britain's Changing Towns** BBC Publications 1967

Perkin, H, **The Age of the Railway** Panther 1970

Pevsner, N, **Pioneers of Modern Design** Penguin Books 1970

Pye, D, **The Nature and Art of Workmanship** Cambridge University Press 1968

Pye, D, **The Nature of Design** Studio Vista 1964

Read, H, **Art and Industry** Faber (fifth edition 1966)

Read, H, **To Hell with Culture, and other essays on Art and Society** Routledge Kegan Paul 1963

Richards, B, **New Movement in Cities** Studio Vista 1966

Rowland, K, **Looking and Seeing** Ginn 1964

Russell, G, **Looking at Furniture** Lund Humphries 1964 (revised edition)

de Sausmarez, M, **The Dynamics of Visual Form** Studio Vista 1964

Stanton, C, **Transport Design** Studio Vista 1967

Sutton, J, **Signs in Action** Studio Vista 1965